Multiculturalism: A Very Short Introduction

VERY SHORT INTRODUCTIONS are for anyone wanting a stimulating and accessible way in to a new subject. They are written by experts, and have been published in more than 25 languages worldwide.

The series began in 1995, and now represents a wide variety of topics in history, philosophy, religion, science, and the humanities. The VSI library now contains 300 volumes—a Very Short Introduction to everything from ancient Egypt and Indian philosophy to conceptual art and cosmology—and will continue to grow in a variety of disciplines.

Very Short Introductions available now:

Available soon:

For more information visit our website

www.oup.com/vsi/

Ali Rattansi

MULTICULTURALISM

A Very Short Introduction

OXFORD
UNIVERSITY PRESS

OXFORD

UNIVERSITY PRESS

Great Clarendon Street, Oxford OX2 6DP

Oxford University Press is a department of the University of Oxford.
It furthers the University's objective of excellence in research, scholarship,
and education by publishing worldwide in

Oxford New York

Auckland Cape Town Dar es Salaam Hong Kong Karachi
Kuala Lumpur Madrid Melbourne Mexico City Nairobi
New Delhi Shanghai Taipei Toronto

With offices in

Argentina Austria Brazil Chile Czech Republic France Greece
Guatemala Hungary Italy Japan Poland Portugal Singapore
South Korea Switzerland Thailand Turkey Ukraine Vietnam

Oxford is a registered trade mark of Oxford University Press
in the UK and in certain other countries

Published in the United States
by Oxford University Press Inc., New York

© Ali Rattansi 2011

British Library Cataloguing in Publication Data

Data available

Library of Congress Cataloging in Publication Data

Data available

Typeset by SPI Publisher Services, Pondicherry, India
Printed in Great Britain
on acid-free paper by
Ashford Colour Press Ltd, Gosport, Hampshire

ISBN 978-0-19-954603-9

1 3 5 7 9 10 8 6 4 2

*In memory of my father, the most successful man
I have ever known.*

Contents

Acknowledgements

The ideas presented in this book have been formed over a long period of time, going back to the late 1980s. I cannot possibly thank all the people who have helped shape and clarify my views. However, for giving so generously of their time and for sharing their ideas with me, I would particularly like to thank Yasmin Alibhai-Brown, Floya Anthias, Avtar Brah, Phil Cohen, James Donald, Anthony Giddens, Jagdish Gundara, Stuart Hall, David Held, Tariq Modood, Maxine Molyneux, Karim Murji, Bhikhu Parekh, Ann Phillips, Ann Phoenix, Nikolas Rose, David Slater, Grahame Thompson, Nira Yuval-Davis, and Sami Zubaida. Sheila Munton of the City University library provided invaluable support. Without Shobhna I would not have had the courage to start the book nor the strength to finish it.

List of illustrations

Introduction

> Individual choice, however tarted up with a thin veneer of
> communitarianism, cannot supply the bonds of recognition,
> reciprocity and connection which give meaning to our lives
> as social beings ... On the other hand we cannot enfranchise
> the claims of community cultures to norms over individuals
> without at the same time expanding – not only ideally but in
> practice – the right of individuals as bearers of rights to
> dissent from, exit and oppose if necessary their communities
> of origin.
>
> (Stuart Hall, 2000)

> Different cultures are to be valued but it is always wrong for
> them to take precedence over fundamental human rights.
>
> (Yasmin Alibhai-Brown, 2000)

In the early 1990s, in *'Race', Culture and Difference*, I published
a critique of both multiculturalism and anti-racism as then
practised in the UK, especially in the field of education.
Multiculturalists, I pointed out, had a simplistic view of ethnic
cultures as homogenous and having static, core, essential
characteristics; and they thought of multicultural societies as 'salad
bowls' with separate, intact ethnic cultures. They also operated
with problematic definitions of racism as irrational prejudice that
could be eradicated by teaching about 'other' cultures as defined

by superficial characteristics such as cuisine and dress. Anti-racists, who rightly pointed out that teaching about other cultures would not tackle the racism embedded in the majority culture, tended, however, to operate with a reductive view of racism as the product of class inequalities and, not unlike the multiculturalists, as the product of a kind of 'false consciousness'.

But in practical terms, the ground was in the process of being dramatically cut from under the feet of both multiculturalists and anti-racists by Mrs Thatcher's government, with the abolition in 1986 of the Greater London Council, which had pioneered some of these policies in education and other areas, and an attendant derision of such aims by some media. Meanwhile, a backlash against its own version of multiculturalism had already started in the Netherlands, while the French, with their commitment to republicanism and secularism, had officially always turned their backs on what they saw as 'Anglo-Saxon' (meaning Anglo-American) excesses in experiments in cultural pluralism and public recognition of multiple ethnicities and faiths.

In this book I have tried to comment on multiculturalism not only in Britain, but wherever possible also in the Netherlands, France, and elsewhere in Europe. Although there have also been significant developments in Canada, the USA, Australia, and even some Asian countries, I have commented on these only very briefly. The book necessarily focuses on Western Europe.

My intention had been to straddle what have become more or less two quite separate fields in the study of multiculturalism. One is based in political theory, discussing issues such as how multiculturalism, with its emphasis on group identities, can be reconciled with the primary role of individual rights in the liberalism that underpins the constitutions of the Western nation states. The other is located in the social sciences and policy studies, with a focus on the nature of ethnicities and other group identities on the ground, the actual character of interethnic group interactions, and the range of policies that have been developed to accommodate and govern the growing cultural diversity of Western societies.

In practice, the two overlap. Policies have to take due account of laws, for example on freedom of speech, which enshrine ideas of individual liberty. Tensions and conflicts between the principles of free speech and group identities and sensitivities have often become serious flashpoints, as in the Salman Rushdie controversy provoked by the publication of his *Satanic Verses*, the murder of the film-maker Theo van Gogh in the Netherlands, and the publication of Danish cartoons of Muhammad. The brevity of this book, however, has set severe limits. A chapter discussing the work of Brian Barry, Will Kymlicka, Bhikhu Parekh and Charles Taylor, some of the most significant political philosophers to have addressed these issues, has had to be omitted. But I have dealt with some of the relevant issues around reconciling individual liberties with recognition of group identities in various chapters of the book.

For the present, I will confine myself to two key points. Firstly, there has been much misunderstanding about the supposed contradiction between group and individual rights. For example, exclusions which allow Sikhs to wear turbans instead of crash helmets are not instances of a form of special treatment which enable group rights to triumph over individual rights. The right to wear a turban instead of a crash helmet is exercised by individuals as individuals, and the group as a whole has no right to force any individual Sikh to wear a turban. The group has been given no rights over individual members. Secondly, as my choice of epigraphs to this Introduction demonstrates, it is my view that supposedly traditional cultural practices cannot be allowed to override considerations of essential human rights and the ability of members of any ethnic group to dissent from the supposed cultural traditions of their ethnic groups. This issue is especially central to my discussion of gender and multiculturalism in

Chapter 2. It follows that there is no room for full-blown cultural relativism in multiculturalism, and indeed any perusal of the writings of multiculturalists will reveal that none of them is guilty of the wholesale cultural relativism of which they are often accused.

Multiculturalism, of course, has had a bad press in recent years, to put it mildly, and the attacks on it that started in the 1980s in Britain and in the 1990s in the Netherlands have now spread throughout Western Europe. The various chapters in this book identify what multiculturalism actually means and assess the complaints against multiculturalism against the available evidence. I have come to the conclusion that most of the charges against multiculturalism as set out in public debates are either misguided or exaggerated when set against evidence garnered from research conducted by social scientists and for governmental inquiries.

It has also become clear that many of the ills attributed to multiculturalism have actually either been caused or exacerbated by what I call a 'triple transition': an unravelling of the nation state, as hitherto placid substate national minorities such as the Scots and Welsh in the UK and the Basques and Catalans in Spain make separatist demands, while the state also loses power to the European Union and global institutions; de-industrialization in the previous urban manufacturing heartlands of major European cities where the initial migrants of the post-Second World War era settled to meet the demands of economic expansion; and retrenchment in previously generous welfare state provisions. Although the question of de-industrialization does receive some discussion, I do not have the space in this book to comment on these transitions in any detail. But all three should always be borne in mind as the essential backdrop against which the narratives and travails of multiculturalism have been played out.

The global financial crisis that began in 2008, and its fallout in relation to retrenchment of public services and higher unemployment, is feeding into even more anxiety for populations already uncomfortable in the maelstrom of increasingly fast-moving dislocations produced by the furious pace of change in what is often described as a period of 'late modernity' for Europe and the West. However, too many of the worries caused by growing economic insecurity, and more general social fragmentation, have been displaced onto issues of immigration. In the process, 'multiculturalism' appears to have become the container into which Western European nations have poured anxieties whose origins often lie in social and economic changes that are considerably wider than those stemming from the consequences of immigration and multiculturalist policies.

For reasons that I shall set out, however, it is also my argument that multiculturalism suffers from flaws that cannot be remedied without moving on to a more sophisticated phase – 'interculturalism' – in the governance of the new multiethnicity, or 'superdiversity' as Vertovec has called it, that now characterizes Western societies. In the context of the triple transition and the global financial crisis, these nation states are now grappling not only with the consequences of migration from their former colonies in the immediate aftermath of the ending of the Second World War and the subsequent economic expansion, but also from displaced populations of failed states and civil wars. There are also the labour demands that flow from the new knowledge economy, the expansion of the financial sectors in a new era of global flows, falling birth rates, and freer labour mobility from European Union expansion and the collapse of the Soviet Union.

Without new, more democratic and egalitarian forms of intercultural governance, the rising tide of the Far Right could become a flood that will severely strain the opportunities for multi-ethnic civility in the period of financial austerity, rising unemployment, and severe cutbacks in public services that we are now entering. In the conclusion to the book, I have been able to sketch out only the beginnings of the rethinking that is required to move on from multiculturalism. Some of the new policies that are required have already begun to take early shape in initiatives that have emerged in the wake of recent 'community cohesion' and 'integration' policies, whatever their shortcomings. The new policies are often based on dubious foundations, ranging from the theory of 'social capital' to the philosophy of 'communitarianism', as well as the demand for loyalty and adherence to poorly specified 'common values' or national identities. But as we shall see, they also contain the seeds of a new era of more adequate policy-making based on a philosophy of interculturalism which demands greater interethnic dialogue and interaction than seems to have been required by most forms of multiculturalism.

At the same time, as my discussion also emphasizes, policies for reducing ethnic disadvantage need to become more effective than hitherto. Encouragement must also be given to every attempt to reign in wider inequalities of class and gender within European nation states and to tackle the global inequalities which will continue to push populations of the South and East to a North ever more reluctant to provide work or refuge except on the harshest of conditions.

Chapter 1
What is multiculturalism?

Perhaps what is clearest in recent public debates about multiculturalism is that not much is clear when it comes to the key terms involved. An acceptable definition of multiculturalism has been notoriously elusive. In turn, proposed alternatives such as 'integration' have also remained vague. It is best, then, to begin with some brief historical and terminological preliminaries to which the discussion will return at various points in the book.

Cultural diversity and multiculturalism

'Multiculturalism' entered public discourses in the late 1960s and early 1970s, when both Australia and Canada began to declare their support for it. That these countries at this time felt the need to embrace the identity 'multicultural' and declare their support for multiculturalism provides important clues as to the general meaning and significance of these terms.

This was the period in which Australia and Canada had begun to allow a new immigration that was now 'Asianizing' these nations. Until then, Australia had a whites-only immigration policy as set out in the Immigration Restriction Act of 1901. Both Asians and Jews were regarded as inassimilable. In 1971, there was an official recognition of the need to assist in the creation of a 'multicultural' society, paving the way for a complete abolition of 'racial' qualifications in 1973.

Immigrants were encouraged to 'integrate' rather than required to assimilate. This meant that they were to be enabled to retain elements of their 'home culture', and ethnic community associations were seen as important vehicles of integration.

I have highlighted the element of integration within multiculturalism, and will do so subsequently, to emphasize that multiculturalism has never been about encouraging separation and segregation. It has involved the creation of structures in which the incorporation of immigrants and ethnic minorities occurs fairly and with the recognition that the desire of immigrants and minorities to retain aspects of their cultures is reasonable, and that cultural diversity is itself desirable and benefits the nation in a variety of ways. Also, as we shall see, it has an equal opportunities and anti-discriminatory strand that is often ignored in debates about the meaning and effectiveness of multiculturalism.

In Canada, the debate began with troubled relations between the English- and French-speaking regions in the 1960s. A Royal Commission on Bilingualism and Biculturalism recommended that English and French be regarded as official languages. But the 1969 Bicultural and Bilingual Act also opened up the question of other minorities in Canada, and the Royal Commission's further recommendation that wider cultural pluralism be added to Canadian identity became established as official policy. This was initially accepted within a bilingual English and French framework, but by 1988 there was a Multicultural Act that widened the terms of inclusion.

Similarly, the arrival of immigrant populations from India, Pakistan, Bangladesh, and the Caribbean islands into Britain and the growing numbers of North African migrant workers in France and elsewhere in Western Europe after the Second World War placed 'multicultural' questions on their public agenda as the immigrant communities began to establish a permanent or semi-permanent presence. While France in particular rejected any policy that gave official recognition to the new immigrants, in Britain a 1966 statement by the then Home Secretary Roy Jenkins set out a general framework for the inclusion, indeed integration, of the new immigrant communities into the British national cultural and polity:

> Integration is perhaps a rather loose word. I do not regard it as meaning the loss, by immigrants, of their own national characteristics and culture. I do not think we need in this country a 'melting pot', which will turn everyone out in a common mould, as one of a series of carbon copies of someone's misplaced vision of the stereotyped Englishman ... I define integration, therefore, not as a flattening process of uniformity, but cultural diversity, coupled with equality of opportunity in an atmosphere of mutual tolerance ... If we are to maintain any sort of world reputation for civilised living and social cohesion, we must get far nearer to its achievement than is the case today.

Note the emphasis on both cultural diversity and equal opportunities.

Multiculturalism and racialization

Despite the wording of Jenkins's statement, it is important to note that the response to the incoming populations all over Western Europe, as well as in Australia and Canada, generally regarded the immigrants as *racially* distinct from the majority white populations, although by then the legitimacy of the idea of 'race' had already been seriously challenged. The issue of multiculturalism was *racialized* from its inception. To a large degree, multiculturalism has its origins in responding to populations that had previously resided in Europe's colonies and which had by and large been regarded as innately inferior races.

s still common practice, in Britain especially, to use
'ial' and 'multicultural' as interchangeable descriptions,
in Germany the racist nightmare of the Nazi period had
public discourse that, officially at least, debated the issues
in terms of the 'foreigner' (*Ausländer*).

In most debates on multiculturalism, in Europe especially, 'race' is the elephant in the room, so to speak. Racism is more often than not the unmentioned and, for many, the unmentionable dark shadow haunting attacks on multiculturalism, to the point that in popular media and culture critiques of 'multiculturalism' often function as a euphemism for hostility to 'coloured immigration' and 'coloured immigrants' of South Asian, African Caribbean, North African, and Turkish descent. The strongly entrenched structure of global inequality may be regarded as the second elephant in the room. It is this inequality that has been the driver for the migrations to Western Europe.

Secondly, and partly because of racialization, the origins of the multicultural debate lie in the perceived difficulties of *assimilating* these newer communities to the host national cultures.

'Assimilation' came to be regarded as difficult, if not impossible, on three grounds: supposed racial distinctiveness which, in practice, related to superficial physiological differences such as skin colour but which seemed to signify an insuperable biological and cultural barrier which, if breached, would end up completely changing the national character; secondly, the obvious hostility exhibited by the host 'white' populations to the 'coloureds'; and finally, the unwillingness of the migrant communities themselves to simply give up all facets of their cultural distinctiveness – for example, language and religion – and somehow become the same as the host populations in all cultural respects.

There has also been another political and cultural trend that has assisted the development of multiculturalism: the growing acceptance within Western liberal democratic states that ethnic minorities have the right to retain their distinctive cultures, although always within certain limits. And arguments about precisely what these limits should be have been at the heart of many debates about multiculturalism. The idea of 'cultural rights', as we shall see, is part of a larger narrative about the emergence of an international human rights agenda.

In the United States, the African Americans' fight against racial discrimination transformed itself into a cultural struggle as well, by asserting a distinct cultural blackness and sense of self-respect typified by the slogan 'Black is Beautiful'. Soon, Mexican Americans and other 'Hispanics', and the long-suppressed indigenous population of American Indians (so-misnamed because Columbus thought he had landed in the Indies), also demanded public cultural recognition as distinct communities separate from the dominant white Anglo-European mix that had come to define American identity. Multiculturalism entered the public vocabulary only in the 1990s with demands for cultural recognition in school and university curricula by these non-white ethnic groups. Thus issues of race have always been significant, and sometimes paramount, in US debates about multiculturalism.

The meaning of multiculturalism: a first approximation

It is not surprising, then, that the dominant meaning that 'multiculturalism' had acquired by the 1980s and 1990s, as set out in the *HarperCollins Dictionary of Sociology* (1991), for example, referred to

> the acknowledgement and promotion of cultural pluralism...
> multiculturalism celebrates and seeks to promote cultural variety,
> for example minority languages. At the same time it focuses on the
> unequal relationship of minority to mainstream cultures.

Thus we also have other important points to note in addition to issues of racialization and assimilation. Multicultural questions are also to do with a celebration of cultural diversity and pluralism, and redressing the inequalities between majorities and minorities. And these are questions of majority and minority *ethnic* groups within modern nation states.

Multiculturalism thus usually refers to policies by central states and local authorities that have been put in place to manage and govern the new multiethnicity created by non-white immigrant populations, after the end of the Second World War. Confusingly, the term 'multicultural' is also used descriptively, to refer to societies that are multiethnic; but the debates considered in this book are about multiculturalism, that is, about the policy response to the diversity created in increasingly multicultural (multiethnic) societies.

Extending the meaning of multiculturalism

In discussing the origins of what one might call the 'turn to multiculturalism', I have referred to several types of minority groups whose existence, growth, and, in most cases, claims and demands have led to the emergence of multiculturalism in modern Western nation states. So far, I have referred primarily to *immigrant* minorities, which would include groups such as the Turks in Germany and South Asians and African Caribbeans in the UK, as well as what has been called a *substate national minority* such as the Québécois, or French Canadians, and also African Americans, who are not a substate national minority but a dispersed, racialized population that was already present at the birth of the American nation state and therefore also quite distinct in origins from immigrants into Western Europe or North America. Moreover, there are other types of minority groups that are also relevant to the general turn to multiculturalism, most especially *indigenous peoples* such as the Maori in New Zealand, the Inuit and First Nations in Canada, the Aboriginal peoples of Australia, and the First Nations in the United States.

Thus, while the most recent debates about multiculturalism have primarily concerned recent immigrants into Western Europe and the USA, and to some degree African Americans, the fact that indigenous peoples and substate minorities have also been relevant means that the description of multiculturalism as involving majority and minority relations must be elaborated to reflect its true complexity.

The point is that the histories and demands of different types of 'ethnic minority groups' vary quite considerably. Substate national minorities such as the Québécois in Canada, the Scots and Welsh in the UK, the Catalans and Basques in Spain, the Flemish in Belgium, and the indigenous peoples mentioned above, have claims that are different from those of recent immigrants such as Pakistanis and Bangladeshis in the UK, Moroccans in the Netherlands, or the Turks in Germany. The national settlements that have been made regarding territorial autonomy, land rights, separate legal and educational systems, and so forth in relation to substate minorities are distinct in many respects from the ways in which recent immigrant minorities have been accommodated in Western Europe, Australia, and Canada.

Given the constraints of space, and the very different histories of Western Europe and North America, I am primarily going to be concerned with the issues and debates concerning the immigrants who have migrated to Western Europe in the second half of the 20th century. The terms of settlement whereby older religious and ethnic populations were incorporated into the nation state has meant that different national cultural, legal, and institutional frameworks were created for minorities, and these have had lasting influences on the reception, treatment, and accommodation of relatively recent immigrants. And these different national trajectories have led to somewhat different versions of multiculturalism. While it is not appropriate to refer to completely different 'national models' of multiculturalism, multicultural settlements in different European nations and in North America have distinctive institutional arrangements.

The international human rights agenda and multiculturalism

The part played by the struggles of indigenous peoples and substate national minorities in the debates about multiculturalism also point to the significance of a larger narrative about the development of multiculturalism. It is possible to see the origins of multiculturalism in a wider struggle for human equality that followed the end of the Second World War, as Kymlicka in particular has pointed out.

The Universal Declaration of Human Rights of 1948 ushered in a new era which in principle distanced itself from pre-1945 ideas of racial, national, and ethnic superiority and inferiority, typified by, and especially identified with, the Nazis against whom the Western allies had fought in their war with Hitler's Germany.

The real novelty of this principle of human equality should be recognized. In 1919, when Japan had tried to introduce a clause regarding human equality into the covenant of the League of Nations, this had been immediately rejected by the Western nations. This is not surprising. The Europeans, after all, were involved in defending empires in large parts of Asia and Africa based quite explicitly on racial principles which deemed whites superior to other 'races'.

As I have recounted in some detail in my book on racism in this series of Very Short Introductions, the discrediting of racial ideas had begun in the inter-war period of the 1920s and 1930s, especially by American anthropologists, a process that gained great impetus from discoveries in the biological sciences, especially genetics. The Universal Declaration of Human Rights, though, marked a major symbolic reversal for racist ideologies and a global political rebuff for movements that championed racist policies.

However, the establishment of an international cultural climate sympathetic to human rights and equality only followed in the wake of sustained struggles on the part of a variety of subordinated groups, including the populations of European colonies.

Of course, the period since the 1960s has been one of myriad social movements and campaigning struggles which have had a profound impact on the political and civic culture of Western democracies. The women's movement, the campaign to transform the status of gays and lesbians, and a growing environmentalism, to mention only the most obvious, have intersected with anti-racism and multiculturalism to create what its critics especially have referred to as a period of 'identity politics'. Claims for cultural recognition have been advanced, which have either complemented the earlier Left and Liberal struggles for wealth redistribution or cut across them and sapped their energies, depending upon the different points of view, which are discussed later.

Varieties of multiculturalism

Although it is not appropriate to talk of different national 'models' of multiculturalism, in part because this implies well-thought-out national variations, it is nevertheless the case that the trajectories of multiculturalism in different countries have varied for a wide range of reasons. Before embarking on a brief discussion of the differences, it is as well to create a foundation for comparison by listing the policies that are generally identified as multiculturalist. Kymlicka and his co-authors have compiled an inventory which is useful for identifying the degree to which countries may be regarded as 'multiculturalist', in the sense of having adopted multiculturalist policies.

The list has been compiled on the basis that multiculturalist policies incorporate two basic principles: firstly, that admissions criteria should be race-neutral, so that immigrants to multiculturalist countries came increasingly from non-European and more often than not from non-Christian, and fatefully, from mostly Muslim countries; and secondly, that immigrants can retain and express their ethnic identities, therefore placing an obligation on the part of public institutions such as the police, schools, media, museums, hospitals, welfare services, and local authorities more generally, to accommodate these ethnic identities. These principles yield eight multiculturalist policies that have been adopted to varying degrees in different countries:

1) Constitutional, legislative, or parliamentary affirmation of multiculturalism at the central and/or regional and municipal levels.
2) The adoption of multiculturalism in the school curriculum.
3) The inclusion of ethnic minority representation and sensitivity in the mandate of public media or media licensing.
4) Exemptions from dress codes, such as allowing Sikhs to wear turbans instead of helmets or school caps, and exemptions from laws banning Sunday trading, and so forth.
5) Allowing dual citizenship.
6) The funding of ethnic group organizations to support cultural activities.
7) The funding of bilingual education or mother-tongue instruction.
8) Affirmative action for disadvantaged groups.

This is not an uncontentious list. Especially, the last item should more appropriately be referred to as the creation of anti-discrimination legislation, such as Britain's series of so-called Race Relations Acts which increasingly barred discrimination against 'coloured' minorities in access to employment, housing, bars and restaurants, and other resources and amenities.

Nevertheless, the list allows a reasonable comparison of the strength of commitment to multiculturalist policies in different countries. On this basis, Kymlicka and his co-authors argue that those adopting 6 out of the 8 policies should be categorized as 'strong' adopters of multiculturalism; those that scored between 3 and 5.5 (the half-mark indicating more tokenistic policy adoption and implementation) should be regarded as 'modest' adopters; and those scoring under 3 are 'weak' adopters of multiculturalist policies.

This classification yields the following grading:

STRONG: Australia, Canada
MODEST: Belgium, the Netherlands, New Zealand, Sweden, UK, USA
WEAK: Austria, Denmark, Finland, France, Germany, Greece, Ireland, Italy, Norway, Portugal, Spain, Switzerland

However, the list gives only the briefest indication of the responses of different nation states to their newer ethnic minorities. Especially, it obscures important institutional differences between the policies of countries in any one category and between categories, does not illuminate the different historical paths of multiculturalism, and therefore also cannot form the basis for any explanation for the differences. And the differences, and reasons for these divergences, are significant. Key influences in the development of different patterns of multiculturalism in European nation states have been existing church–state relations and what have been called 'citizenship regimes', as we shall see.

The more widespread adoption of multiculturalism in Australia and Canada has been attributed to their search for what has been called a 'founding myth' of the kind that is elsewhere supplied, for example, by the US's self-conception as a nation of immigrants, or the ethnic and religious identities that make up a significant part of the national narrative of other states such as the UK, the

Netherlands, and Sweden. This has also meant that in Canada and Australia the conception of a positively multiethnic, multiculturalist nation has been fostered as an identity for the whole nation. In most European states, in contrast, multiculturalism has often been primarily aimed at integrating the ethnic minorities as a subordinate, sometimes very minor, part of the national narrative. In some countries, this is no doubt part of an imperial legacy in which, despite the close relationship between colonial subjects and the metropolis in the formation of the metropolitan nation state, the role of the colonies economically and in key wars and in culture and so forth has always been hugely devalued, a point I shall come back to.

And an examination of the different historical trajectories of multiculturalism in Britain and the Netherlands, for example, in the context of their histories before the immigration of the second half of the 20th century is crucial in enabling a proper understanding of the differences between them that are obscured by simply labelling both as 'modest' adopters, as in the grading exercise attempted by Kymlicka et al.

The Netherlands: 'pillarization', polarization, and integration

The Dutch created a system in which the newer ethnic minorities, who came from the previous colonies of Indonesia and Surinam as well as Turkey and Morocco, were given considerable cultural autonomy and resources with which to retain their cultural identities. By 2000, nearly 9% of the population was foreign-born and 17% had at least one foreign-born parent. Already by 1980, it had become clear that most immigrants were going to stay – belying the hope that they were 'guest workers' who would eventually return home – and the Dutch government developed what it called an 'Ethnic Minorities' programme of policies. Minorities were given even more resources to retain their mother tongues and their cultures via support for their own newspapers and separate channels on television. In doing so, the Dutch were following a well-worn national path in the governance of different cultural groups within the nation. They had an already institutionalized structure of 'pillarization', involving separate cultural spheres, which from the 19th century onwards had allowed Protestants, Catholics, Jews, and different politically inclined groups – Liberals and Socialists – to live peaceably together, but with the minimum of contact between them. By the 1960s, pillarization had lost much of its relevance, as Entzinger has pointed out, because of the forces of secularization, especially, but also general individualization. But the effect remained particularly strong in education. Even in recent times, only one-third of Dutch primary schools are state schools, the rest being privately run either by religious groups or those having particular educational perspectives.

The more explicit policy towards the newer ethnic minorities from 1983 onwards had as its objective 'achieving a society in which all members of minority groups in the Netherlands, individually and in groups, are in a situation of equality and have full opportunities for their development', or what commonly became known as 'integration with retention of identity'.

However, the particular history of 'pillarization' in the Netherlands meant that the minorities policy did indeed lead to more formal institutional separation than in other countries, with the minorities being given greater freedom and resources to develop their own schools, newspapers, broadcasting facilities, and cultural associations.

The Dutch rarely referred to their policies as 'multicultural', a fact confirmed in my private exchanges with the distinguished scholar Han Entzinger. Even in the 1980s, with a more explicit encouragement of pluralism for the newer minorities, the initiatives were called 'ethnic minority' policies. It was only in retrospect, and often from outside the Netherlands, that the policies were referred to as 'multiculturalist'. Ironically, the Dutch version, heavily influenced by the previous history of consociational democracy or pillarization, is the only one of all the European multiculturalisms that can be genuinely charged with fostering separation between ethnic groups, the accusation now habitually levelled at all forms of multiculturalism.

The shape of the backlash in the 1990s against the ethnic minority policies in the Netherlands prefigured the form it has taken in other European countries. Overall, the policies were criticized for failing to integrate the ethnic minorities both economically and culturally. It was felt that insufficient proficiency in the Dutch language and lack of familiarity with Dutch society had been particularly strong obstacles. As a result, new immigrants were required to attend new language and civic integration courses, the conditions for which became more draconian in the new century, with immigrants required to finance the courses at their own expense, and responsibility for integration being shifted more strongly to the immigrants themselves. At the same time, though, there was an official recognition of the Netherlands as an immigration country and a multicultural society.

As Prins and Saharso have pointed out, the critics also initiated what came to be regarded as a timely 'new realism'. This was framed in a perspective that posited an absolute difference between Western liberalism, with its principles of free speech and secularism, and the repressiveness of, especially, Islamic minority cultures. In part, this was informed by events outside the Netherlands, especially the Salman Rushdie affair in Britain. This polarization was allied to the charge that permissiveness towards minority cultures had allowed them to separate themselves off from mainstream Dutch society – a lament echoed subsequently in much of Europe – and had also made them more welfare-dependent.

The reaction against the ethnic minorities policy gathered force, as elsewhere, after 9/11. In the Netherlands, this was given special impetus initially by the rise of Pim Fortuyn's *Leefbaar Nederland* party and his attacks on the welfare state, European unification, Islam, liberal toleration, the liberalism of the Church, and the continual arrival of other immigrants and asylum-seekers. The controversy provoked by his popular interventions was later given further fuel by the assassination in November 2004, by a Muslim, of the film-maker Theo van Gogh (more on this later) and the threats against his co-documentary-maker and member of parliament, Ayaan Hirsi Ali, herself a Muslim immigrant and fierce critic of Islam.

The intensity of anti-immigrant and anti-Islamic rhetoric has been toned down since 2007, and there has been a more compassionate policy towards asylum-seekers, no doubt influenced by the fact that the Netherlands was condemned by the European Council and Human Rights Watch for violations of the rights of asylum-seekers and immigrants. However, the rise of the virulently anti-Islamic Freedom Party has now introduced a further destabilizing dynamic into Dutch politics.

The UK: 'race', 'essentialism', and the changing politics of recognition

In the case of Britain, there is an oft-repeated shorthand history that suggests that the country treated its post-1945 immigrants from its former colonies – and many that were still colonies until the 1960s – rather like it had treated them when they were 'natives' in the colonies. That is, as Favell puts it:

> Britain ruled by letting the natives be as they were, civilizing [sic] them through ... institutions that were ... often modifications of the ones they found in the native culture ... Britain saw its Empire as a dominion of generic British civilization in which all the cultures of the world could flourish under the never-setting sun.

But more sceptical commentators have also added that the British learned much about divide and rule policies in conquering India and Africa, and the advantages of co-opting local leaderships to subjugate colonial populations, and then domesticate the colonial and post-colonial immigrants it imported to augment the labour force in post-war reconstruction. Moreover, the British Empire had also fostered notions of Britain as the 'mother country', a notion that was naively believed by many West Indians in particular as they boarded first the *SS Windrush* in 1948 and then other ships to fill the unskilled jobs, especially in declining industries, that white Britons had begun to shun in favour of better-paying, less onerous, and more skilled employment.

The idea of Britain as a mother welcoming her overseas children seemed to be borne out by the 1948 Nationality Act which had granted citizenship and free entry to all from the colonies and the self-governing white Dominions of Australia, New Zealand, and Canada.

But as I have also recounted in some detail in my *Racism: A Very Short Introduction*, all was not what it seemed on the surface. We now know from the archives that the 1948 Nationality Act which guaranteed citizenship and free entry was actually put in place to allow whites from the Dominions to come and settle or travel to and fro as they wished. There was little inkling that those who would take the opportunity would be 'coloureds' from the West Indies, India, and Pakistan. The British Labour Government tried to prevent the *SS Windrush* from sailing because the preferred policy was to recruit white Polish and other displaced East Europeans. When the ship sailed anyway, Colonial Office civil servants were sent to the West Indies and India to prevent any further migrations, and every attempt was made to convince would-be migrants that there were no jobs in Britain.

But the growing National Health Service and a desperate London Transport soon began recruiting drives in the West Indies and

1. West Indian immigrants arriving at Victoria Station, London, 1956

India. Eager employers in manufacturing industries in the North, Midlands, and London also snapped up migrant workers, leading to 'chain' migrations as news about employment opportunities reached the West Indies, India, and Pakistan. As with such colonial and post-colonial migrations into the Netherlands and France, even skilled workers were forced to take the unskilled, dirty, and dangerous jobs, and those involving night shifts, which white British workers were able to spurn in a booming economy. And the 'coloured' immigrants found cheap housing in poorer neighbourhoods, their choices not only constrained by income and the desire to send money home, but also by direct discrimination against them by private landlords and public authorities.

The common usage of 'coloured' and 'black' in the UK, not to mention more insulting slurs such as 'wog', are symptomatic of the more explicit racialization of the vocabulary and attitudes with which the newer minorities have been governed, compared to elsewhere in Europe. While the Netherlands has always had an ethnic minorities policy, the British have framed issues in terms of 'race relations'. A key 1969 report by Rose was uncontentiously entitled *Colour and Citizenship: A Report on British Race Relations*. 'Multiracial' and 'multicultural' continue to be used synonymously.

However, this racialization of public discourse, which has the unfortunate effect of giving legitimacy to the wholly discredited idea of 'race' and allows a space for the baggage of racial ideology of innate white superiority to stay just under the surface, has also been accompanied by ever-stronger anti-discrimination measures, referred to as Race Relations Acts (the first in 1965) which have been far in advance of measures in the rest of Europe. One of the most significant was the Race Relations Act of 1976 which recognized unintentional and indirect discrimination as requiring reform and redress. Of course, given that races do not actually exist, anti-racist legislation faces difficult dilemmas about how 'racial groups' are to be defined. It is worth noting that under the influence of civil rights struggles in the USA, anti-racist activists in Britain had readily adopted the race-inflected category of 'black' to unite both South Asians and African Caribbeans in a joint struggle to fight discrimination in employment and public services, a strategy that eventually collapsed as Asians developed myriad ethnic associations and addressed issues around immigration and service provision that were of more specific concern to them.

Long-discussed plans for restricting 'coloured' immigration were finally implemented from 1962 onwards with Commonwealth Immigration Acts and Nationality and Citizenship legislation which choked off further immigration, except family unification, from the so-called new Commonwealth. This basically distinguished the 'coloured' post-colonials from the whites of the Dominions of Australia, New Zealand, and Canada. The 1981 Nationality Act was also significant for ending the practice of *ius soli*, or the automatic granting of citizenship to children born in the UK of non-citizen parents.

British multiculturalism, then, has always had a self-consciously twin-pronged approach which has married 'integration' of the immigrants already in the country with strict restrictions on further 'coloured' immigration.

That Britishness has a white racial connotation has been hotly disputed by the mainstream media, already hostile to multiculturalism, and even by Centre-Left politicians generally sympathetic to multiculturalist initiatives. This became clear in the public furore over just this suggestion by the Parekh report on *Multi-Ethnic Britain* published in 2000. But there is an important truth in this insight. Britain's multinational state, uniting the English, Scots, Welsh, and Northern Irish, under English cultural hegemony, has always found it difficult to grant the status of 'English', 'Scottish', 'Welsh', or 'Irish' to its non-white citizens, who have to find an identity within an ill-defined 'Britishness'. British Asians and British African Caribbeans are made acutely aware of this non-acceptance by the question that a brown- or black-skinned person routinely faces: 'But where are you really/ originally from?' or 'But where are your ancestors from?' The identity of 'Paki' or 'nigger' regularly and rudely overrides claims of genuine belonging by people of Asian or African origin, and the conflation of 'multiracial' and 'multicultural' means that in Britain, opposition to immigrants and immigration is often expressed through opposition to 'multiculturalism'.

Multiculturalist and anti-racist initiatives in schools and the delivery of local authority services, especially, together with the setting up of community associations for ethnic minorities, often wholly or part-funded by the minorities and many with sympathetic provision of buildings by local authorities, began to suggest that important cultural transformations were perhaps beginning to take root. Nationally, what began as the Rampton Report into West Indian under-achievement in schools became the 1982 Swann Report which recommended the implementation of multicultural schooling for all. Urban disorders involving black youth in London and the Midlands in the 1980s put black urban disadvantage, under-achievement, and unemployment squarely on the public agenda, especially as the Scarman Report into the Brixton disorders in London blamed general disadvantage and inequalities, rather than institutional racism amongst the police and other agencies, for the frustration and anger amongst black youth.

Hopes of serious multicultural progress suffered serious blows under the Thatcher government elected in 1979. The recommendations of the Swann Report were shelved. A National Curriculum with a strong emphasis on white British history and a Christian ethos was imposed. Repeated central government and media attacks on Labour-controlled local authorities with a strong public commitment to multiculturalism, especially in London, and which usually had Leftish leaderships, led to the phrase 'loony Left councils' becoming firmly embedded in the national consciousness as a byword for supposedly insane proposals to impose forms of 'political correctness'. As media researchers subsequently pointed out, the tabloid press even invented stories, such as the ones about proposals for banning the phrase 'black dustbin liners' or the children's nursery rhyme 'Baa baa black sheep'.

Symbolically, the most powerful move against multicultural and anti-racist initiatives was the Thatcher government's abolition in 1986 of the Left-leaning Greater London Council (GLC) under Ken Livingstone which had formally put an anti-racist ethos at the centre of its radical agenda for promoting equality, especially in education, allied to initiatives informed by feminism and a more militant egalitarianism in relation to class inequalities.

The more radical anti-racism of the GLC variety also began to alienate liberals. A division opened up between self-styled 'anti-racists' and those derided by them as 'multiculturalists', again particularly evident in conflicting perspectives on interventions in schools. The anti-racists, often identified with the Institute of Race Relations, questioned whether the liberal multiculturalist policy of teaching about 'other cultures' could ever effectively mount a direct challenge to racist attitudes and practices, pointing out that knowledge about minority cultures did not address the issue of racism within the majority culture. In any case, as the critics argued, the teaching about minority cultures was trite and superficial, focusing as it did on giving white children exposure to Indian and West Indian cuisine, music, and forms of dress – which came to be called the 'saris, samosas, and steel drums' syndrome. This was seen as simply diversionary activity by the anti-racists.

Moreover, as the critics of these early attempts at introducing multiculturalism pointed out, they were underpinned by an unacceptable level of 'essentialism'.

Most students of multiculturalism have now come to recognize that cultural essentialism is one of the biggest obstacles to a constructive debate about multiculturalism, while also hindering the creation and implementation of multiculturalist policies. Many forms of multiculturalism, including ones that were being developed in British schools and in social services provision, did operate in an 'essentialist' manner, that is, with simplistic versions of ethnic minority cultures and a tendency to see them as having a small number of unchanging key characteristics and as being tightly bounded entities – which has been called the 'billiard ball' syndrome. Anti-racists and other critics were quite right to point up this deficiency. Conservative critics who argued from a more assimilationist viewpoint, on the other hand, operated with essentialist versions of the Britishness into which immigrants were supposedly to be assimilated, an issue that is addressed mainly in Chapter 5.

At a national level, multiculturalist and anti-racist initiatives continued to be rebuffed throughout the 1990s when the

Conservatives were in power in Britain. To take just one instance, in January 1997 the John Major government vetoed European Union plans to set up a European Monitoring Centre on Xenophobia and Racism which was going to mark the launch of the European Year Against Racism. It was with the arrival of a Labour Government later that year that progress was made on such issues. The new government also allowed Britain to have European-agreed human rights legislation and an inquiry into the murder of black teenager Stephen Lawrence, which exposed deep-seated cultures and practices of racism within the London Metropolitan Police that had allowed the murderers to escape prosecution.

However, the situation was different at many local levels. While many cities in the North of England used the Conservative years to do little in terms of multiculturalism, a negligence that was soon to be clearly exposed in the wake of widespread urban disorders in 2001, cities such as Leicester quietly continued to invest in a wide range of school and community measures which have now come to be praised as models of their kind. Many London boroughs also continued with multicultural measures, such as the printing of leaflets in several languages and continuing with what was referred to as 'race awareness' or 'diversity' training for workers in health and social services. There is evidence to suggest that some Labour-controlled local authorities in London, Birmingham, and Leeds, especially, provided community resources to minorities in order to ensure their vote in elections, and that the minorities were aware of their electoral clout and exploited it. This also led to divisions within communities becoming more entrenched, and gave excessive powers of patronage to those who, for a variety of reasons, became accepted as 'community leaders'. Critics of multiculturalism in Britain, such as Malik and Hasan, have highlighted this uneven process in an attempt to discredit the whole of multiculturalism as a distraction from genuine struggles to redress ethnic and wider inequalities. But it is also clear that there was a genuine, although variable, commitment to ensuring that ethnic disadvantage was tackled and that there was an integration of ethnic minorities via thriving local associations and other forms of what the distinguished Canadian philosopher Charles Taylor was to call the 'politics of recognition' in 1992.

Misgivings about essentialism amongst many radical anti-racists and general egalitarians were often allied to the criticism – perhaps most eloquently expressed by the American writer Todd Gitlin – that the drive to establish multiculturalism, together with the development of other 'new social movements' such as feminism, gay rights, animal rights, and environmentalism, had led to a form of 'identity politics' which distracted attention and energy away from the 'real' struggle to reduce class inequalities. Sometimes the debate was played out in slightly different terms via the accusation, most famously made by another American, Nancy Fraser, that multiculturalism and anti-racism were primarily struggles over 'cultural recognition', which undermined or cut across the more important need to fight for redistribution of material resources, fears echoed in Britain by commentators such as Malik. Both charges were misleading. The Gitlin-type critique not only failed to understand that even class conflict involved social identities, but also that there had previously been an over-emphasis on class at the expense of inequalities of gender, sexuality, and ethnicity, and that these were not trivial side issues but required urgent redress and which in the process would produce a deepening of democracy and more egalitarian social relations generally. Meanwhile, as many commentators – Parekh perhaps most succinctly – pointed out, redistribution and recognition are not opposed but inherently intertwined, requiring each other in strengthening the overall goals of greater economic equality and wider cultural expression and diversity.

The self-styled British anti-racists, as I pointed out in an essay in the early 1990s, also relied on reducing racialized inequalities and racism too much to class in various forms. This meant that, although their critique of the essentialism of the multiculturalists was well taken, a move away from their class reductionism was also necessary if more sophisticated strategies were to be put in place of the damaging divisions that had opened up between the anti-racist and multiculturalist camps. I also argued that questions of gender, including masculinity, also needed to be addressed by incorporating the concerns of feminists. Some of this critique had been foreshadowed in the 1989 Report into an inquiry into the murder of an Asian schoolboy at the Burnage High School in Manchester, where the school's anti-racist policy had been criticized for an excessive moralism, for neglecting to involve white working-class parents in the policies, and a failure to address the widespread masculinist culture of violence, all of which had contributed to a situation that led to the murder. The failure to involve whites generally has eventually led to strong resentment, as multiculturalism has been viewed as privileges for black and Asian people at the expense of whites, rather than as an attempt to combat ethnic socioeconomic disadvantage as well as cultural exclusion from the nation's self-identity.

The outbreak of widespread violence in cities in the North of England in 2001 marked a watershed and had a huge influence on successive Labour governments, first elected in 1997. The disorder was widely blamed on multiculturalism and its supposed effects in allowing ethnic minorities to lead 'parallel lives'.

A new integrationism, similar in many respects to the Dutch about-turn discussed earlier, increasingly took hold in Britain. A new era of 'community cohesion', supposedly the opposite of multiculturalism, had begun to take shape. I discuss this in some detail in Chapter 4.

For the present, it is worth noting that both in the Netherlands and in Britain the forms of multiculturalism that developed were very much pragmatic, top-down creations with little genuine public debate and involvement from the majority or the minorities, a liberal paternalism that has often found itself rudderless and panicked in the face of explosions of popular resentment or senses of injustice from below. There is considerable truth in Yasmin Alibhai-Brown's sarcastic jibe:

> White Britons were failed historically by the political elite who did not prepare them for the changes that came after the war – and who still give out mixed messages about whether immigration has been a good thing for this nation. One moment people in Britain were being taught that they were the imperial masters who had the God-given responsibility to civilize the barbarians they controlled – the next minute these black and Asian people were in the work canteen demanding to be treated as equals. White Britons were told that black and Asian immigration was a threat but at the same time they were instructed to treat those already here as equals.

France: secularism, immigration, and *de facto* multiculturalism

The public face of the French state and its local authorities is one of implacable hostility to the curiously mis-named 'Anglo-Saxon' approach, supposedly typified by the USA and Britain, of public recognition of ethnic minorities, a commitment to the flourishing of minority cultures, and the general celebration of cultural diversity and multiethnicity.

The French approach is particularly influenced by its conception of secularism. French secularism, or *laïcité*, involving the formal separation of church and state, received important codification in the famous Separation Law of 1905, after a circuitous journey for the laicization process which guaranteed freedom of religious worship but banned the placing of any religious 'sign or emblem' on public monuments, although the state agreed to fund chaplaincies in schools and prisons. French *lacité*, like all secularisms, has always been open to different interpretations and institutional expressions. Fetzer and Soper distinguish between 'strict' and 'soft' versions which have held sway in different periods and in different sectors of the state and amongst clergy, educationalists, and politicians. In the strict version, which is supported by teachers' unions, feminists, and the 'Republican Left', praying in public, refusing to eat certain foods in school canteens, and wearing religious clothing or jewellery are all regarded as violations of *laïcité*. A softer version, popular amongst those on the 'multicultural Left', human rights activists, and many Christian, Jewish, and Muslim leaders, supports the state funding of religious or faith schools, encourages dialogue amongst faiths, and advocates students' freedom to express their religious identities in schools as long as they respect religious pluralism. They also argue that the strict version of *laïcité* violates international law and human rights covenants.

In recent years the different versions of *laïcité* have come into play in the various Muslim headscarf, or *hijab*, controversies that I discuss in some detail in the next chapter.

France experienced, and indeed encouraged, high rates of immigration from other European countries such as Poland, Italy, Spain, and Portugal throughout the period before the end of the Second World War. These waves of immigration had two features that distinguished them from the flows that started from the former French colonies of North Africa after 1945. Firstly, the European immigrants were not racialized and therefore were not regarded as posing any problems of assimilation. This allowed France to continue regarding itself as a country in which immigration played no part in its self-identity. Secondly, the Communist Party and its trade unions played an important role in organizing and integrating the immigrants, and in doing so, encouraged the formation of separate ethnic collectivities and ethnic political machines which endured for a considerable period even after the Second World War.

However, the non-European, non-Christian immigrants from the colonies of the Maghreb were treated as racially other and more or less inassimilable. As late as 1969, the Calvez Report for the Economic and Social Council recommended that the state should treat workers from the Maghreb as 'temporary' workers only linked to specific labour needs and that their entry should be controlled by a process involving formal cooperation with the country of origin. Also, the Communist-controlled municipalities that had previously treated European immigrants on the basis of a 'tradition of solidarity', regarded the new immigrants as temporary residents who must be encouraged to return home. As Hargreaves, Schain, and others have pointed out, this even extended to the practice of setting quotas in housing and schools for those of North African origin. Thus, as Schain puts it, the Communists continued to treat immigrants as collectivities, but this time 'in an exclusionary manner'. The term 'immigrant' was exclusively applied to non-whites. Arabic language classes were organized in schools through agreements with the countries of origin. And in June 1974 all non-European Community immigration was stopped, although, as with restrictive measures in the UK, family unification was allowed.

Hostility to the immigrants was tempered by Left attempts to involve the state in ethnic recognition and mobilization in the 1980s. But in general the Republican model remained in place, one further consequence of which was that the policy of not giving official recognition to ethnic minorities, for example in the census, has also continued.

The bulk of the immigrants from the Maghreb were Muslims, and they have found themselves doubly handicapped. The French both racialized them and had a strong tradition of ambivalence and hostility to overt expressions of religious identity that have clashed with Muslim practices of public religiosity.

In practice, the French state has also practised a form of *de facto* 'multiculturalism', however abhorrent the term has been. A 1981 law lifted the restrictions on North African immigrants that had prevented them from creating ethnic associations along the same lines as European immigrants. Such organizations mushroomed, and by the end of the 1980s there were at least 3,000 of them, acting as intermediaries with trade unions, local authorities, and political parties. At least 1,000 were overtly Islamic, while others, such as *SOS-Racisme*, were more broad-based. The state also set up zones of educational priority (ZEP) in poorer urban areas which, as in the Netherlands, Britain and elsewhere, were also where immigrants had been forced to settle, and where there had been a series of disorders in the 1980s and 1990s involving immigrant youth.

The contradiction between the public rhetoric of universalism and opposition to multiculturalism and the actual practice of the state is nowhere more clearly illustrated than in the 1990 invitation to representatives of Muslim organizations to form a Deliberative Council on the Future of Islam in France. Subsequently, the government has funded training institutes for imams in an attempt to create a French Islam free of foreign influences. In 2003 a nationally representative central Muslim council was set up, the *Conseil Français du Culte Musulman*.

The continuing controversies over the *hijab* point to the persistent tension in French public culture between pragmatic concessions to ethnicity and public religiosity and the desire to maintain the tradition of Jacobin Republicanism. The rise of militant international Islam, widespread urban disorders in the 21st century involving the young descendants of North African immigrants, mostly Muslim, in protest at unemployment and heavy-handed policing – discussed in more detail later – and the need to liaise with the flourishing ethnic associations, have all kept various forms of *de facto* multiculturalism alive.

It seems clear that governments of both Left and Right have come to the conclusion that the best course of action for France is to find ways of combining the recognition of cultural difference with the traditions of French Republicanism. However, that compromise still does not involve the asking of ethnic questions in the census. The actual numbers of ethnic minority citizens is still a matter of informed guesswork. Whether this is a viable basis for social policy remains a divisive question in French public life.

November 2010 saw a potentially significant development, for the French Office for National Statistics issued the first official figures on discrepancies in employment patterns between French citizens with immigrant parents and those with French parents. French men with parents from the Maghreb had an employment rate of 65% compared with 86% for those with French parents; the comparable figures for women were 56% and 74%. The statistics office acknowledged that discrimination potentially played a large part in the difference. And in an equally significant move, President Sarkozy announced the abolition of the Ministry of Immigration and National Identity, admitting that it had led to 'tension and misunderstanding'. The setting up of the Ministry had come under criticism from historians and other intellectuals, and from the Left, for stigmatizing immigrants and suggesting that citizens with foreign parents were somehow a threat to the nation. This move came soon after legislation had been passed banning the full veil from all public places.

Germany: an 'ethnic' nation comes to terms with the demands of citizenship

Germany had inherited from the early 19th century and even more from the draconian *Volk*-nationalism of the Nazi period a conception of formal citizenship as well as a more general cultural sense that only those of proven German descent could really belong to the nation. Throughout the period from the 1950s to the early 1970s, whilst millions of foreign workers from Italy, Greece, Portugal, Turkey, and Yugoslavia came to Germany, the citizenship policy remained one of strict *ius sanguinis*, descent from 'blood'. This meant that millions of 'ethnic Germans' from all over the world were given automatic rights of citizenship, but the foreign workers had no route to citizenship, and Germany became notorious for its 'guest worker' policy of making foreign workers travel to and fro as the economy demanded. Of the 14 million 'guest workers' in 1973, some 11 million left in the wake of the oil crisis and the recession. But nearly 3 million Turkish workers stayed and, with the support of German and international courts, were able to bring their families to join them. Germany now has some 7.5 million residents of foreign origin, 9% of the population, and some estimates put it at 14 million.

Tentative changes to citizenship law were begun in the 1990s, with a belated recognition that Germany had to abandon its claim that it was not a country of immigration. More fundamental changes were introduced by the citizenship legislation of 2000 and the Immigration Act of 2005, marking an ever more explicit acceptance of guest workers as German.

Not surprisingly in a nation with such a powerful ethnic self-conception, multiculturalism has never had wholehearted official endorsement and has never acquired serious popular support. German Turks have often called for greater moves towards multiculturalism and the celebration of diversity, but even the Greens, who were initially sympathetic, appear to have turned their backs on the idea, although they continue to argue for the benefits of immigration and diversity. In October 2010 the German Chancellor Angela Merkel declared that multiculturalism had 'utterly failed'; this is ironic, given that multiculturalist policies have hardly been tried.

On the ground, in response to local circumstances, a number of concessions has been made, especially in cities such as Frankfurt and Stuttgart which have large populations of immigrant origin. Frankfurt has had an Office for Multicultural Affairs since 1989. It has acted as an advocate for anti-discrimination measures amongst local authorities, campaigns for tolerance and acceptance of diversity, and provides mediation and conflict-resolution services. At the state level, there have been measures to improve the educational performance of immigrant-origin children and especially to facilitate German-language acquisition. Minority mother-tongue teaching remains a marginal enterprise in the education system. The constitutional guarantee of religious freedom and the federal structure have given room for some variation in policies, although the building of mosques and the wearing of headscarves by Muslim women continue to provoke hostility and opposition. The growth of marriages between Germans and those with foreign citizenship, reaching a figure of 16% in 2000 compared to 4% in 1960, are taken by commentators such as Karen Schönwälder as generally hopeful signs of a more bottom-up acceptance of cultural diversity.

The notion of 'interculturalism' has acquired some currency in Germany, and much more so than multiculturalism, with attempts at encouraging interaction and dialogue between minorities and the majority. This is a development about which I will have more to say in the conclusion to this book.

I do not have the space here to provide comparative material on Austria, Denmark, Sweden, Italy, and Spain. Vertovec and Wessendorf's collection *The Multiculturalism Backlash* is particularly useful in providing information on these countries.

Conclusions

Several conclusions stand out from any informed survey of immigration and multiculturalism in Western Europe in the second half of the 20th century. A stark and, for many, an uncomfortable truth is that non-white immigrants from the poorer regions of the world, mostly colonies and ex-colonies of the Western imperial powers, were not welcome and nor were they hospitably received. The otherwise radical Labour government elected in Britain in 1945 was dismayed by the news that the *SS Windrush*, carrying amongst the West Indian passengers many in fact who had fought for Britain in the war, was about to set sail for the UK. Frantic attempts were made to stop it from sailing, and messages were sent out to the rest of the colonies and the newly independent India and Pakistan that there were no jobs available in Britain. The French tried to treat their North African immigrants as guest workers. The Germans, with ethnically restrictive citizenship laws already in place, created a strict guest-worker system which the French, British, and Dutch governments would probably have liked to establish. The tradition of 'pillarization', in any case, allowed the Netherlands to keep non-white immigrants at arm's length from mainstream Dutch society, and governments and large swathes of the white population of Western Europe hoped that the immigrants would only stay for a while.

Hungry for labour, the manufacturing industries of Western Europe and the public sectors, especially transport and health, ignored their governments and recruited heavily from the colonies and former colonies. But, and this is the second conclusion, these workers, whatever the level of their educational and vocational qualifications, found themselves employed in the unskilled and undesirable jobs that white workers were able to shun in booming economies. Discriminated against by private and public landlords, they found cramped rented accommodation in the poorer urban areas. European imperial entanglements in Arab countries and the Indian subcontinent meant that a large proportion of the migrants were of Muslim origin, although at the time this was not thought to be significant.

More important was the deeply embedded racialization that Western European societies had inherited as part of the imperial legacy. This meant that the 'coloured' workers were treated quite differently from the European migrants from Italy, Spain, Portugal, and Poland who had previously fed the labour markets. The non-Europeans encountered a widespread sentiment that they were inferior and almost impossible to assimilate. The doors had been shut on further such labour immigration by the mid-1970s.

Thirdly, the multiculturalism that eventually emerged in an attempt to create an ethos of acceptance and celebration of the cultural diversity created by the new multiethnicity has constantly had to battle against the imperial legacy of racism. Western Europeans have been reluctant hosts to non-white immigrants and reluctant multiculturalists.

Fourthly, multiculturalism has been largely a top-down project, although many trade unions, political party activists, and anti-racist organizations have tried to mobilize on a popular level and have kept up the pressure for fair treatment and awareness of the benefits of the new cultural diversity. The top-down approach has created resentment, which in turn has led to a white backlash.

The critique of multiculturalism has not only come from conservative nationalists. As I have indicated, from the Left many voices have argued that multiculturalist thinking and policies have been weakened by failing to tackle racism head on, that they have succumbed to a simplistic ethnic essentialism and have failed to combine appropriately with general egalitarian struggles to fight socioeconomic inequality.

And official and popular opposition in countries such as France, Germany, Italy, Austria, and Denmark has meant that multiculturalism is still very unevenly developed in Western Europe. The 21st century has seen the emergence of a backlash against multiculturalism. Note, though, that despite many popular pronouncements to the contrary, multiculturalism has never been about encouraging separate development between ethnic minorities and the majority. The aim has always been to create fair-minded, non-discriminatory routes to cultural and socioeconomic integration.

Multiculturalism has now to cope with new patterns of immigration and the emergence of what Vertovec has called 'superdiversity'. This is a consequence of the freer mobility of labour with the expansion of the European Union, the collapse of the Soviet Union, the arrival of asylum-seekers fleeing failed states, civil wars and the effects of Western interventions in the Middle East, the demands of the new knowledge and financial sectors for highly qualified workers, and declining birth rates.

As I write, the election of Far Right members of parliament in Sweden confirms that even this haven of social democracy and liberal asylum policies is following the European pattern of

2. **Island of Samos, Greece, August 2009. Greek coastguards arresting asylum-seekers, most of whom come from Afghanistan, Iraq, Iran, Eastern Europe, Algeria, Morocco, and Palestine**

acute hostility to the new forms of immigration in deindustrialized cities such as Malmö. The backlash against multiculturalism has gained new momentum.

I argue in the Conclusion that multiculturalism as a paradigm and institutional framework needs to move on to forms of interculturalism if it is to cope with the new situation. The coming period of acute financial austerity, however, by reducing resources for public services, increasing the levels of unemployment, and creating higher levels of inequality, will pose a severe challenge even to the more sophisticated form of interculturalism and the recommendations for redistribution that seem necessary.

Chapter 2
Is multiculturalism bad for women?

If the origins of multiculturalism can be traced back to the human rights revolution of the second half of the 20th century and the subsequent emergence of progressive social movements including feminism, it might seem odd at first sight to suggest that multiculturalism might be bad for women. But it would only be strange if movements for rights, recognition, inclusion, and redistribution always neatly dovetailed into each other to form a harmonious whole.

There is in fact no necessary reason why claims for rights on behalf of diverse groups should *not* come into conflict with each other. After all, the feminist movement itself partly came into existence because of dissatisfaction with the 1960s Left and alternative cultural movements which championed working-class interests and new youth cultures but failed to recognize and challenge the societal subordination of women that was also embedded and taken for granted in the practices of the Left and alternative culture movements.

The position of women in any multicultural framework has become something of a litmus test for the acceptability of multiculturalism. Ironically, even many social and political conservatives, not especially noted for their sympathy for women's rights and advancement, have often opportunistically used the gender issue to bolster their case against multiculturalism.

It has reached the point, as some commentators have noted, that in so far as multiculturalism may be said to be in crisis, more often than not, it is being played out on the bodies of women.

How can multiculturalism be bad for women?

The central issue at stake is easy to spell out. If multiculturalism involves support for the survival of ethnic minority cultures and their traditions, and if these traditions in fact disadvantage women, then multiculturalism is clearly bad for women and should not be endorsed by anyone who believes in the equality of women and men.

Western nation states, although premised on the formal equality of women and men in the public sphere – employment, political organizations and assemblies, education, and so forth – in fact are far from equal when measures of income, occupational status, membership of representative assemblies, and other indices are taken into account. Indeed, feminists and egalitarians in the West quite rightly continue to highlight these inequalities and to campaign against them. But the intertwining of the gender question with the critique of multiculturalism has largely tended to focus on the practices of ethnic minority communities of non-Western origin now living in Western nation states and on the subordination of women in non-Western societies. The reason is that many of these communities, or some parts of them, do not even accept the formal equality of women and men.

A number of non-Western practices have come under the spotlight and have generated considerable controversy. Chief among these have been the wearing of headscarves, veils, and other garments by Muslim women; the practices of arranged and forced marriages; polygamy; and female genital mutilation or cutting. We will examine all of these in this chapter.

And as we shall see, the question of gender also raises other fundamental issues: of how minority 'cultures' are viewed, often in stereotypical and essentialist terms; the relationship between cultures and individuals; and the rights of individuals *vis-à-vis* 'their' cultures.

The strong incompatibility thesis

The argument that there exists a fundamental tension between women's rights and multiculturalism has been most forcefully and clearly put by the late American political scientist Susan Moller Okin in a widely discussed essay whose title I have used for this chapter: 'Is multiculturalism bad for women?' she asked, in an article first published in the journal *Boston Review* in 1997. Her answer was an almost completely unequivocal 'yes', although she did subsequently tone down her initial espousal of what I have called the 'strong incompatibility thesis'.

Her arguments have had a wide resonance amongst many feminists and liberals who have had reservations about what they have seen as a modish but ill-judged enthusiasm for the multiculturalist policies, practices, and principles adopted by many Western nation states from the 1970s onwards.

Okin was convinced that what she called the granting of group rights, which she regarded as intrinsic to multiculturalism, worsened the position of women in the patriarchal cultures of ethnic minorities in Western nation states. By allegedly treating the minority cultures as 'monoliths', and thus ignoring internal power differences between women and men, and even more so by the tendency to treat any intervention in the private sphere of family and domestic life as incompatible with preserving the group's way of life, multicultural policies helped to perpetuate the subordination of women in these communities.

Taking issue with multiculturalist notions that the self-respect and freedom of minority groups lay in being able to preserve their own cultures, Okin suggests instead that women in these minority cultures

> *might* be much better off if the culture into which they were born were either to become extinct (so that its members would become integrated into the less sexist surrounding culture) or, preferably, to be encouraged to alter itself so as to reinforce the equality of women – at least to the degree to which this value is upheld in the minority culture. (emphasis in original)

Okin comes to this much cited and controversial conclusion on the basis of a survey of minority cultures, in which she highlights the prevalence of a variety of practices which seriously disadvantage and harm women and contribute to their distress and continuing subordination to men.

First, polygamy: she points out not only that the French in the 1980s allowed many to immigrate with more than one wife, leading to over 200,000 polygamous families in Paris by the late 1990s, but also of course that polygamy is an obvious example of men's interests and desires predominating over those of women. She cites evidence from the countries of immigration into France that women there have little liking for polygamy, and also that men see it as a way of disciplining women: if a wife 'misbehaves', she can be threatened with the arrival of another wife.

Second, she highlights the practice of rape leading to marriage. In Latin America, parts of Southeast Asia, and West Africa, rapists can be legally exonerated of the offence if they marry the victim.

Third, she refers to what in the USA has been called 'cultural defence' in the criminal courts. For example, Hmong have attempted to defend their traditional practice of marriage by 'kidnap and capture' in this way. Another 'cultural defence' practice she cites concerns mothers of Japanese and Chinese origin who have killed their children and have also tried to kill themselves after the shame of the *husband's* infidelity.

Finally, she points to the practice of clitoridectomy, also commonly referred to as female genital mutilation or female genital cutting, which is performed among some ethnic minority groups, especially those of West and East African origin, in the West. Okin points out that the justifications provided for the practice are quite clearly against women's interests: clitoridectomy is practised to limit women's sexual pleasure, thus encouraging virginity before marriage and sexual fidelity after marriage. Women who get no pleasure from sex are more likely, so the justification for clitoridectomy goes, to stick to their roles as mothers, cooks, and wives.

Of course, Okin shows an awareness that many ethnic minority women are also willing participants in the perpetuation of these practices that oppress women, but her view is that to regard this as a defence is to ignore the fact that much sex discrimination is hidden in the private, especially the family, sphere, where 'culture instills' in women and 'forces' upon them particular social roles.

Okin's critics

Ironically, given Okin's view that multiculturalists tended to ignore internal power differentials in ethnic minority communities, she herself has been vulnerable to the criticism that her own treatment of these communities misses their internal complexity. Okin sees these communities as entirely separate, internally integrated wholes that are essentially constituted by women's subordination (a tendency also evident in more recent critics of multiculturalism such as Hasan who attack multiculturalism for its essentialism and then present ethnic minority cultures, especially Asian cultures, in caricatured and stereotypical terms).

In keeping with this type of essentialism, the critics point out, Okin focuses almost exclusively on extreme cases of the subordination and sexual abuse of women such as female genital mutilation, rape, and murder, thus falling into the trap of stereotyping the minority communities in a crude and unhelpful manner. In doing so, she also stereotypes ethnic minority *women* as largely passive victims.

The Okin-type portrait of ethnic minority communities, again a common feature of anti-multiculturalist critiques, also has the unfortunate and misleading effect of creating a sort of rigid binary opposition between the West and the Rest, with the West (or 'us') being represented as lovers of liberty and equality while the Rest ('them') are painted as uncivilized, barbaric 'others' with scant respect for women's dignity and rights.

Feminist anthropologists and ethnic minority women activists – sometimes being the same persons – paint a more nuanced picture of women's positions and activism in the cultures condemned by Okin.

Female genital mutilation

There is little agreement as to how long forms of female circumcision have been practised. Nor is it clear in how many countries it is common practice today. But historically, it does appear to have been practised in ancient Egypt and was not uncommon in 19th-century France, England, and the USA (there is some evidence of it being practised up to the 1950s), where clitoridectomy was prescribed for treating 'hysteria', 'lesbianism', insanity, and epilepsy (presumably without success). At present, it is most prevalent in some African countries, but also to some degree in parts of the Middle East, India, Sri Lanka, Indonesia, and Malaysia.

Female circumcision provokes strong revulsion and is now banned in all Western countries. In September 2001 the European Parliament adopted a resolution on female genital mutilation (FGM) which calls on the member states of the EU to pursue, protect, and punish any resident who has committed the crime of FGM, even if committed outside the EU, and calls on the member states to recognize the right to asylum of women and girls at risk of being subject to FGM. FGM is specifically criminalized in Belgium, Denmark, Norway, Spain, Sweden, and the UK, while in other countries such as France it is dealt with under more general legislation. It is also banned in Australia, Canada, New Zealand, and the USA. Only the USA has allowed fear of FMG to be grounds for asylum.

Legal provisions are often made available in Western countries for women to undergo genital surgery if the appearance of their genitals is causing them considerable mental distress. Male circumcision is usually available in all Western countries, and not only for Muslims and Jews, although there is no agreement on its health benefits or possible ill effects on sexual pleasure.

While the custom of female genital cutting is widely condemned in the West, it is not clear how much popular understanding there is of the variety of practices that fall under this general heading. The least invasive and harmful version involves removal of the prepuce and tip of the clitoris. For some, this is no different from male circumcision, and they argue that as long as this is performed under appropriate medical conditions, it should be allowed.

Two other versions involve more drastic surgical interventions. In clitoridectomy, the clitoris and part or all of the labia minora are removed. Infibulation – also referred to as 'Pharaonic circumcision' – consists of removal of the clitoris, the labia minora, and part of the labia majora, as well as the stitching up of the two sides of the vulva.

It is unusual to find any serious defence of any versions of female genital cutting in the West, and indeed the common use of the term 'female genital *mutilation*' is indicative of the widespread opposition to all versions of the practice. It is thus disingenuous of critics to use FMG constantly as a stick with which to beat multiculturalists and portray them as dangerous cultural relativists who are prepared to put women's health and lives at risk because they are unwilling to challenge supposedly important 'traditions'.

Estimates suggest that worldwide, some 100 to 130 million women have undergone one or other version of the procedure, and that every year approximately 2 million girls and women are circumcised, many illegally in the West. An unknown number of girls are taken abroad to have the procedure and accompanying ceremonies performed.

The American cultural anthropologist Richard Schweder and others have undertaken surveys of the research on FMG and claim that health risks have been exaggerated, that there is considerable evidence that women continue to obtain sexual pleasure despite circumcision, and that there are no grounds for imposing Western aesthetic norms on communities, for example, in and from Sudan, Somalia, Chad, and Mali that prefer a 'smoother' look to female genitals. If breast implants for purely cosmetic reasons are acceptable to Westerners, it is argued, so should labial surgeries be allowed for other women who freely chose to have them.

But few Western multiculturalists are swayed by such arguments. Witness Parekh's very firm and unequivocal rejection of female circumcision, in terms that also display his commitment to universalism rather than the cultural relativism of which multiculturalists are often accused:

> The practice deeply offends against some of the basic human or universal values as well as the operative public values of liberal society. It inflicts irreversible physical harm, is sexist in nature, violates the integrity of the child, makes irreversible decisions for her, and removes an important source of pleasure. It therefore deserves to be banned unless its advocates offer compelling reasons that measure up to its enormity.

He also points out that it has no religious sanction, for it is not mentioned in the Qur'an; and the *hadith* – traditions derived from other of Muhammad's utterances – contain only an ambiguous and passing reference.

In many cases, the degree to which female circumcision is firmly embedded as a custom in 'traditional' cultures can also be doubted. In Senegal there was a successful campaign against female genital cutting when *Tostan*, a local non-governmental organization, realized that the main reason villagers held on to a practice they knew to be painful and dangerous was the almost certain expectation that their daughters would become unmarriageable if they were the only family refusing to circumcise their daughters. Women from *Tostan* initiated a collective pledge which ensured that all villagers would abandon the practice on a specific date. It appears that the pledging soon gained momentum; more and more villages gave up female circumcision after 1997, and in 1999 the government was able to introduce legislation banning the practice of female genital cutting.

While this example shows that it is easy to over-estimate the commitment of 'traditional' communities to a practice of this kind – and thus, as Ann Phillips argues, that the support for genital cutting in this case requires no special theory of cultural difference – there is little doubt that female circumcision does have strong support amongst women in many African ethnic groups.

And this raises the issue of whether adult women living in the West who want to undergo the procedure in their countries of origin should be allowed to do so. Schweder and others including Parekh cite many cases of highly educated women of African origin living in the USA or Europe who are keen to be circumcised, especially after marriage. Should a sane adult woman of Kenyan origin and a citizen of the UK be prevented from undergoing a properly supervised circumcision in Kenya?

It is as well to note that we if are going to grant agency to women and assume that they do not mindlessly play out a culturally given script, then their choices deserve respect; in which case, with Parekh, one should hold that the sane adult woman who wants to undergo such a procedure in her country of origin should be allowed to do so.

But she cannot legally do so as a resident of Western countries.

However, given this ban, some – including the women affected – may be tempted to argue that it is not multiculturalism that is bad for women, but an inflexible, culture-blind approach. But how much can a sane adult person be allowed to harm herself in the name of 'culture', assuming that we can ascertain the degree of harm that will be caused by a particular form of female circumcision?

Whatever the answer one might give in the face of this dilemma, there appears to be a growing international consensus that female genital cutting as usually practised is a serious hazard to health and constitutes a violation of human rights. And the practice has now been banned in many African countries including Benin, Burkina Faso, Chad, Egypt, Ghana, Guinea, Kenya, Niger, Nigeria, Senegal, Tanzania, and Togo, and there have been prosecutions in many of these states. In Sudan only the most extreme form, infibulation, is banned, although there is evidence that it continues to be widely available.

Given that no Western country allows female genital cutting, and very few multiculturalists support the practice, if multiculturalism is bad for women, it is not because of any multiculturalist sympathy for FGM, whether based on cultural relativism or other grounds.

Forced marriages and 'honour' killings

The issue of forced marriage became especially publicly visible when Danish legislation in 2002, aimed at preventing forced marriages amongst minority communities, stipulated that any Danish citizen wanting to marry a foreign citizen could do so only if both partners were 24 years of age. And they also had to prove that their connection to Denmark was stronger than their connection to another country, which illustrated the way in which the issue of forced marriage had become intertwined with the anti-immigration agenda as well as the backlash against multiculturalism.

However, in Danish debates there appears to be no serious consideration of any distinction between *arranged* and *forced* marriages. Arranged marriages, widely practised in minority communities whose origins lie in South Asia – Indians, Pakistanis, and Bangladeshis – tend to involve consensual practices in which both families play a significant part in bringing couples together. However, it is important to be aware of the degree of informal pressure that often exists on each would-be spouse in arranged marriages, and it is noteworthy that British South Asians tend to marry early, a trend influenced by parental and 'community' pressure.

Forced marriages often involve teenage girls born in Western European countries being lured to Pakistan or elsewhere on pretence of a holiday and then forcibly married off to a cousin or other person connected to a clan or village of the girl's family. In some cases there are straightforward abductions, and the girls are unwillingly taken abroad. Marriages also take place in the UK and elsewhere in Western Europe where the girl is simply married off against her will, often accompanied by threats of violence and pleas for maintaining 'family honour'.

All the available evidence suggests that forced marriages, whilst they definitely occur, are a minority practice amongst ethnic minorities and have been widely condemned by their cultural and religious leaders. And in the UK, for example, ethnic minority women's groups have been at the forefront of the fight against this practice. Southall Black Sisters, established as early as 1979, and Newham Women's Project and Muslim Women's Helpline have campaigned vigorously against forced marriages and violence against women, and have provided protection and advice to hundreds of women who have managed to seek help or have had their cases taken up by these organizations.

The British Home Office set up a Working Group on Forced Marriage in 1999 which included a prominent member of Southall Black Sisters. In 2005 what had become a Community Liaison Unit was turned into the Forced Marriage Unit. It seems that in cooperation with the British High Commission and police forces in India, Pakistan, and Bangladesh, some 200 or so individuals who had been taken there by families for marriage are repatriated annually. Also, the minimum age for overseas marriages has been raised to 18 for both partners.

Moira Dustin and Ann Phillips of the London School of Economics Gender Institute highlight several important features of these activities. Firstly, that practice has shifted from an earlier reliance on mediation by family members and community leaders to a greater support for the young women (and they are overwhelmingly women) as individuals; secondly, that little help can be provided for those forced into marriages in the UK; thirdly, that the focus on overseas marriages means that the issue gets entangled with questions of immigration rather than being included in measures to deal with the wider issue of domestic violence; and fourthly, that in creating a two-tier system whereby only those marrying outside the EU have to wait until the age of 18, the regulations may be helping to perpetuate a damaging stereotype 'representing [minority] parents as intrinsically more coercive, and the young people as intrinsically less able than those from majority groups to exercise autonomy or know their own minds'.

To what extent have multiculturalist policies or sentiments been guilty of colluding in the practice of forced marriages as many critics have claimed?

In the late 1960s and 1970s, there is evidence of a somewhat culturally relativist tendency in court judgements in the UK. The Court of Appeal revoked a care order on a 13-year-old Nigerian girl in 1969 despite her marriage to a 26-year-old husband, on the grounds that such marriages were 'entirely natural' in Nigeria where the marriage had taken place, although what had happened would have been abhorrent to 'an English girl and our Western way of life'. In 1975 widows of 'potentially polygamous' marriages were judged to have rights to a widow's pension despite the fact that these marriages were not recognized in British law; in this latter case, arguably, the cultural relativism worked in favour of women.

But as the success of campaigns by women's groups such as Southall Black Sisters and the activities of the Forced Marriage Unit show, the tide has turned against such irresponsible cultural relativism.

The same is true of other Western European countries, such as Norway. An earlier willingness to sympathize with what have been called cases of 'cultural defence' has given way to more rigorous responses to calls for help from girls of Turkish and other ethnic minority origin who fear forced marriage.

On the other hand, in many countries, most notably Denmark, but to some extent in the UK as well, the forced marriage issue has been deliberately hijacked to suit anti-immigration agendas, with age restrictions on the potential spouses and the introduction of citizenship tests serving to restrict immigration, especially from outside the EU. And there is little doubt that in the popular imagination, especially via the tabloid press and other media, an exaggerated reporting of the issue of forced marriages has tended to reinforce views of non-Western minority communities as uniformly backward and unable to integrate. Far more of the UK's population will be aware of forced marriages than the existence of, say, the Southall Black Sisters who have had such an impact on fighting this practice and influencing state policies.

The increasing unwillingness of the European states to allow cultural defence in favour of forced marriages is a welcome move towards support for individuals against pleas for maintaining supposed cultural inheritance and customs advanced by dubious guardians of equally dubious 'traditions' usually practisced by a small minority within the ethnic minority communities.

What is true of forced marriages is also true of the horrific practice of 'honour' killings, a term that acts as a fig leaf for the (often premeditated) murder of young women who have supposedly brought 'shame' to the honour of families. In the UK, although formal governmental initiatives began in 1999, it was only in 2003 that the Metropolitan Police Service set up the Strategic Homicide Prevention Working Group on Honour Killings which, amongst other things, began a programme of training for staff who would be involved in the investigations.

Thoughtful commentators such as Dustin and Phillips have pointed to the dilemmas inherent in interventions by police and other agencies. If 'honour' crimes are treated as separate from other forms of domestic violence, there is a danger of stereotyping minority communities as more accepting of domestic violence, and an unhelpful distinction can become entrenched between crimes of 'honour' characteristic of the East and crimes of passion associated with the West, with the added overlay of regarding minority individuals as more determined by 'culture' and those from the majority as subject to individual aberrations. There is a danger, too, that all instances of domestic violence and abuse in minority communities may be portrayed misleadingly as 'honour' crimes.

However, the existence of properly informed and trained staff in a specialist unit may be more likely to ensure that cultural stereotypes do not prevent imminent danger from being recognized, and the pleas of young women for protection from being heard. And this is not necessarily to underplay the fact that male violence against women is hardly just a minority practice; on average, two women a week are killed in the UK by current or former partners and spouses, with the majority of murders being perpetrated, of course, by men from the majority communities, and often for supposed sexual misbehaviour.

Of course, all state interventions can become hostages in other kinds of reforms. As researchers Hege Skjeie and Birte Siim have discovered, in Norway and Denmark, for example, a focus on 'honour' crimes, forced marriages, and FGM has allowed the issue of limited ethnic minority representation in public bodies such as parliament to be marginalized; and, as mentioned earlier, the radical Right has used gender concerns to bolster its campaigns against immigration. In the Netherlands, social researchers Baukje Prins and Sawitri Saharso argue that although the public discourse has tended towards regarding minority – especially Muslim – women as passive victims and as colluding with activities such as 'honour' crimes, in practice there is greater awareness that the gender issues are not only 'cultural' but have socio-economic dimensions.

It is arguable that this more sophisticated approach has only emerged as a result of the abandonment of multiculturalism in the Netherlands. But it signals a new phase of more sophisticated multiculturalism, one that more pragmatically combines multicultural sensitivities with an awareness of related issues of poverty, unemployment, and a greater emphasis on 'integration'.

In any case, it is all too easy to exaggerate the supposed excesses of multiculturalism when it comes to charges of cultural relativism in connection with violence against women in ethnic minority communities. Anne Phillips concludes her survey of the degree of acceptance of so-called 'cultural defence' in crimes against women in ethnic minorities with the view that

> I do not...see much evidence that something called
> multiculturalism is encouraging the courts to let men from minority
> cultural groups off the hook for acts of violence against women.

Rather, she argues, courts have tended to be lenient to men from all groups, including the majority, when they plead mitigation because the women partners they have attacked have slept with other men or women, or have simply wanted to end the relationship.

The French headscarf wars

The headscarf, initially referred to as the *foulard* in French but later more so as the veil (*voile*) or *burka*, and also often conflated with the *bilbab*, or full-length dress combined with headscarf, are all regarded as signs of the inequality of women under Islam and therefore incompatible with French traditions of sex equality.

In July 2008 France denied citizenship to a *burka*-wearing woman of Moroccan origin on the grounds that her 'radical' practice of Islam was indicative of her acceptance of inequality between the sexes; in turn, this meant that she was insufficiently 'assimilated' as she was supposedly rejecting a basic French value of sex equality. (The *burka* in this case refers to clothing which covers the head, face, and body, leaving only the eyes visible.) In appealing against a similar ruling against her in 2005, the 32-year-old woman, known only as Faiza M, a good speaker of French, married to a French national, and having three French-born children, had invoked the French constitutional right to religious freedom. She had claimed that she had not been wearing the veil in Morocco. But French social services had reported that 'She lives in total submission to her male relatives'. In October 2010 the full veil was banned in public.

The French decisions raise a number of crucial issues that go to the heart of debates about the relationships between women, multiculturalism, national identity, and religion – especially Islam – that have been the key themes of this chapter. The French, in contrast to the British, Dutch and others, have been militantly secular and also strongly opposed to multiculturalism. They have consistently maintained that the garments such as the headscarf are external signs of religion which cannot be worn in schools, although in principle adult women are allowed to wear them; they are interpreted as external signs of religion in a public institution that not only go against the French tradition of *laïcité* but are said to be indicative of the way in which a multiculturalism that would allow girls to wear these veiling garments would be colluding in their oppression.

The headscarf has been an issue in other European countries, but to nothing like the same extent as in France. My discussion focuses on the French case because it reveals some of the more general paradoxes and contradictions that lie at the heart of debates around multiculturalism and assimilationism and their consequences for women. At the same time, it is part of the whole wider question of how and under what terms former colonial subjects and others are to be allowed to become fully accepted Europeans, and to what extent European nation states are able to understand and challenge the continuing elements of racism which disfigure their cultures.

By 1993 the French had already changed the rules of nationality. Citizenship would no longer be automatically granted to children born in France to foreign-born parents; instead, these second-generation residents would have to formally apply for citizenship, thereby signifying their *individual* desire to enter into a social contract, leaving behind all communal loyalties.

But the 1993 codes of nationality revealed the extent to which Muslims and Arabs – regarded as equivalent despite the fact that not all French Muslims were Arabs, and not all Arabs were Muslims – had fallen foul of a number of rigid binary dichotomies which had become part of the framework within which the French discussions of the place of citizens of Muslim-Arab origin had been taking place: tradition/modernity; barbarism/ civilization; identity/equality; (Muslim) patriarchy/(French) gender equality; religious fundamentalism/secularism; communalism/individualism; multiculturalism/national unity; assimilability/inassimilability, amongst others.

It is important to remember that although the French debate has been particularly polarized around these oppositions, echoes of them can be found in all the European countries, including the UK, which have been agonizing over multiculturalism and the place of Muslims in particular. The simple headscarf, a common enough form of apparel for European women well into the 1950s, and a continuing part of the Frenchwoman's wardrobe, as the American researcher John Bowen points out, has become an extraordinarily potent symbol for a much wider anxiety of a 'clash of civilizations' between the West and Islam. As Bowen puts it, 'It is never just about scarves.' When women of North African origin first began to settle in France in the 1960s and 1970s, there was little controversy about the fact that some of them wore headscarves, 'a common Mediterranean costume, little different from that worn by Catholic women in the south of Italy, Spain, or France itself'.

As is usually the case, the simple oppositions which imprisoned the debates over-simplified and distorted the cultural realities on the ground, especially with regard to the identities, motivations, and social position of Muslim women. And as Joan Scott argues, in the process the French managed to displace attention away from the real and urgent issues of inequality, racial discrimination, and socio-economic marginalization that face its former ethnic minority citizens, including the women. Or as Bowen has it, the French actually seemed to *blame* the headscarf for a large number of French problems, including anti-Semitism, Islamic fundamentalism, growing ghettoization in the suburbs, and the breakdown of order in the classroom.

The cultural binaries around which the controversies became organized were intertwined and overlapped, hence their public power. This also means that any discussion of them must necessarily treat several of them together at any one time.

Take the question of tradition versus modernity. The headscarf became a symbol of the French Muslim population's attachment not only to tradition as opposed to modernity, but to a backward, uncivilized culture; and one of the signs of its backwardness was its unacceptable patriarchy which supposedly forced girls and women to wear the headscarf.

The simmering question of the headscarf first erupted into public controversy in October 1989 when three schoolgirls were expelled from their middle school in Creil, some 30 miles from Paris, for refusing to remove their headscarves. Note that the school was in a deprived and ethnically mixed special educational priority zone, or ZEP, which was described by its principal, a black Frenchman with origins in the Antilles, as a 'social rubbish pail'.

But were the girls making a (patriarchally forced) stand for fundamentalist Muslim religious tradition against modern French secularism? And was this part of what the principal, Eugene Cheniere, was later to call an 'insidious jihad'? Were the girls motivated by a desire to bring about an Iranian-style Islamic revolution? The answers to these questions appear to be definitely in the negative.

It became clear when the girls' own voices were finally heard that they had made the choice to wear the headscarf *against* the wishes of their parents. And two of them were persuaded to take them off in the classroom only after an intervention by the king of Morocco, which came after pressure from French Muslim community leaders on the girls to comply with the demands to conform to France's *secular* norms. Moreover, surveys indicated that even more than ten years later, only a small minority of between 10% and 15% of Muslim women wore the *hijab*, although a majority said they actively practised their religion.

Thus, not only was it difficult to interpret the girls' choices as forced upon them by traditional Muslim patriarchal culture and the men in their families and communities, but it also became clear that the wearing of the headscarf was very much a minority practice amongst French Muslim women. Nevertheless, as many commentators have pointed out, the public debate in France tended to see in the girls' actions a generalized rejection by all French Muslims of France's secular ideals and of the French tradition of gender equality. Even the case of the Jewish Levy sisters, who converted in 2003 in the teeth of opposition from Leftist parents and grandmother, made little difference to the prevailing stereotypes of why Muslim girls wore the headscarf.

Of course, there were dissenting French voices. Catholic and some Protestant and Jewish leaders argued that secularism did not mean the complete silencing of religious expression. The sociologist Olivier Roy interpreted the actions of the various Muslim girls as analogous to those of their non-Muslim young counterparts who were seeking spirituality in an age of extreme secularism and materialism. In this and other senses, Roy sees the current rise of Islam as a product of and a reaction to Westernization, not a simple throwback to 'tradition'. Other French sociologists also saw a generational divide, pointed to religion as a way for a marginalized group to assert its identity, and all of them pointed out that the girls were not committed to radical Islamic politics, something which in any case had only minority support amongst French Muslims (as elsewhere in Europe).

The Stasi Commission recommended in its report *Laïcité Republique* that in keeping with the principles of French secularism all 'conspicuous' signs of religious belonging, such as headscarves, the Jewish skullcap, or yarmulke, and the Sikh turban, could not be worn in public schools; at the same time, it called for a more inclusive general approach to religious practices and even recommended the creation of Muslim chaplaincies in hospitals and prisons, alternatives to pork and fish in school, prison, and hospital canteens on Fridays and the recognition of Yom Kippur and Aid-El-Kabir as national holidays. In the event, the only recommendation that formed part of new legislation in 2005 was the banning of headscarves and other prominent displays, even though previously a variety of compromises such as scarves on shoulders had been pragmatically negotiated.

Just as in debates in other countries where domestic violence was interpreted as an individual aberration but 'honour' killings were seen as culturally determined, so in France the miniskirt was seen as an individual decision that had nothing to do with the cultural pressures of fashion, but the headscarf came to be interpreted as a cultural phenomenon, and indeed one that was the result of an Islamic culture in which women were uniformly oppressed by oversexed men. The huge variety of Islam and the fact that so-called 'veiling' was a minority practice was ignored in a tide of sentiment that pitted the French Republic against Islam.

In ignoring all nuances, the French not only managed to homogenize Islam but also distorted their own history of secularism, and mythologized the unity and progressiveness of French national culture. Despite the official separation of Church and state, the French state, as I have pointed out in an earlier chapter, has supported and financed Catholic, Protestant, and Jewish organizations, including schools. And official aid has also been given for the building of Muslim mosques and graveyards. Arguably, the challenge posed by the desire of Muslims to blur the private/public division only served to exacerbate the contradiction that has been evident in the dominance of Catholicism in a supposedly secular culture. Moreover, although Muslim girls' headscarves were supposedly transgressing against a 'traditional' French Republican value of gender equality, this ignored the fact that the same Republicanism's emphasis on the abstract individual citizen had actually prevented women from acquiring the vote until 1945.

In addition to the misleadingly posed issues of secularism and gender equality, the significance of the various headscarf controversies appears also to lie in the role assigned to the school in the formation of French Republican culture, the perceived challenges to French national culture which became particularly evident from the 1980s onwards, most specifically the diminution of national sovereignty following greater European Union integration and the growing pace of globalization under American (and therefore English-speaking) hegemony, and the growing alarm over radical Islam both globally and within the borders of France. All this was overlain by often virulent racialized hostility to the youth involved in regular and persistent protests and disturbances in the deprived suburbs of French cities.

In resisting the assertion of French Muslim identity as symbolized by the headscarf, the French assumed that they were halting the communalization and fragmentation of French national identity which they blamed on the influence of Islam. However, French sociologists – whose voices were ignored by the Stasi Commission in favour of the views of militant secularist philosophers and historians, as Bowen shows – have repeatedly pointed out that the ghettoization and fragmentation involving France's Muslim immigrant populations has little to do with their (highly variable) commitment to Islam.

As we have seen, the real reason for ghettoization lies in the French government's policy of deliberately housing the immigrant workers it was encouraging to come to France after the Second World War in large, poor suburbs or in industrial enclaves where there was no attempt to incorporate them into the mainstream of French culture. In fact, there was a conscious effort to teach their children the 'languages and cultures of origin' so as to ease their anticipated return to the countries of origin. That is, there was a deliberate attempt to prevent assimilation. And the emphasis on individualism which prevented any official gathering of statistics on the fate of these communities meant that there was no official check on, or recognition of, the gross racial discrimination and consequent racialized deprivation that was being embedded in the outer rims of the cities.

Note one very significant implication for debates in the UK and elsewhere about multiculturalism and its supposed role in creating fragmentation: as is particularly evident in the case of France, the real driving force behind the formation of separate communities has not been 'multiculturalism' but racial discrimination, strongly aided and abetted by official policies. I will come back to this issue.

The implication of the well-documented analyses of Joan Scott and others is that strong anti-Islamic racism has created a double bind for French citizens of Muslim origin. On the one hand, and in line with the official ideology of assimilationism associated with French Republicanism, the only way communities of recent immigrant origin can have a legitimate place in France is by way of thorough-going integration into French culture; however, on the other hand, Islam is seen as essentially and immutably opposed to gender equality (and the headscarf is interpreted as obviously indicative of gender inequality). It is also seen as irredeemably non-French in its rejection of secularism (despite the variety of secularist Islamic nations and the wide acceptance of forms of secularism amongst French Muslims). There is, too, a strong underlying assumption that Islam is and always will be an inferior form of civilization. Therefore *any* adherence to Islam renders the individual inherently un-French and forever incapable of fully and properly assimilating or integrating into French culture.

It is particularly notable that French debates have tended to marginalize the findings of French sociologists that the reasons given by the minority of French schoolgirls who do wear the headscarf are hard to interpret as signs of allegiance to radical Islam or a passive acceptance of the inferior status of women. Some French schoolgirls have tried to make this point by wearing the headscarf in France's national tricolour and bearing one or more words from the French Republican proclamation of '*liberté égalité et fraternité*'. The wearing of the headscarf is in fact part of a much more complex process in which the inability of contemporary France to provide genuine socio-economic opportunities and a sense of belonging to its Muslim population has had an important role. It is also part of the process whereby second- and third-generation French women of Muslim origin are trying to find ways of accommodating their allegiance to Islam with their equally strong desire to belong to French culture.

3. French Muslim schoolgirls demonstrating in the streets, their headscarves proclaiming their commitment to both French identity and Islam

Of course, the issues around anxieties of social fragmentation, the dilution of national culture and identity, and the fear of a growth of radical Islam are not unique to France. All the available evidence suggests that the wearing of the headscarf in the UK, Germany, the Netherlands and elsewhere in Europe, and the reactions to it from the authorities and the wider population, has more than an echo of the same national anxieties, effects of the socio-economic location of minority communities, and the search for new forms of belonging by Muslim populations, both women and men. But in most other European countries the accommodation between the Muslim woman's headscarf and national cultural traditions has been a less fraught affair.

The complexity of the identities of young Muslim women who wear the headscarf is exemplified by two striking illustrations. First, the case of Remona Aly and her friends in Britain who wear the headscarf but are fans of rock music, from Led Zeppelin and U2 to Muse and Bon Jovi, and find in the music an expression 'of their angst of not belonging – something women in *hijab* relate to'. But it also makes them surer of their 'Britishness', she adds. And then there is 28-year-old headscarf-wearing Asmaa Abdol-Hamid in Denmark, a town councillor, who describes herself as a feminist, a democrat and a socialist, has gay friends, opposes the death penalty, and supports abortion rights. As a newspaper describes her, she is 'a tolerant Scandinavian and European'. But she refuses to shake hands with males on religious grounds. And in the mostly secular, democratic movements in the Middle East from 2011, *hijab*-wearing women of all ages played a prominent part in the demands for political freedoms and popular representation. Go figure, as the saying has it.

Chapter 3

Has multiculturalism created ghettos and 'parallel lives'?

Riots, reports, and terrorism: 2001 and after

The summer and autumn of 2001 were to prove fateful and, some might argue, fatal for multiculturalism in Britain and the rest of Europe. May, June, and July of 2001 saw ferocious civil disturbances in the northern English 'mill towns' (so called because they had previously had thriving textile mills) of Burnley, Oldham, and Bradford. Street battles raged between British Asian youth, mostly Muslim and of South Asian origin, white youth – many belonging to the Far-Right British National Party – and police. Firebombs damaged several buildings. In Oldham these included the somewhat ironically named 'Live and Let Live' pub as well as the home of the Asian deputy mayor.

The British government immediately commissioned a series of official investigations into the disorders and set up its own Home Office committee to liaise with the inquiries, collate the findings, and serve as an advisory body. Bradford had already set up its own inquiry under Sir Herman Ouseley before the disorders, having experienced disturbances in 1995. The Ouseley Report was published first, in the summer of 2001, which in my view meant that its terms of inquiry and conclusions probably had an undue influence on the framework of the other inquiries and on the central government approach to the whole set of issues thrown up by the disorders. As Ousely pointed out in his foreword to the Bradford Report, his 'Race Review' team was given the brief to enquire into why 'community fragmentation along social, cultural, ethnic and religious lines' was occurring in Bradford. In other words, 'the problem' had already been identified before any serious investigations had actually started: 'community fragmentation', used interchangeably with 'community fracturing'. And 'self-segregation' was also identified before the investigation as a key causal factor. The Race Review team was also asked to give advice on tackling racial discrimination and promoting equal opportunities. The inquiries into Oldham and Burnley, together with an independent review under Ted Cantle, could not but bear in mind the Bradford terms of reference and conclusions. The Bradford and all the other inquiries were also working in the shadow of the McPherson Report on the murder of the black teenager Stephen Lawrence in South London which had found deep-seated institutional racism amongst the police and had produced a set of wide-ranging recommendations for tackling racism and related issues.

However, the investigating teams were also well aware that they faced a complex set of circumstances. Overall, despite inevitable differences of emphasis, several common themes emerged in their attempts to highlight essential background factors and the more immediate triggers to the disturbances. As we shall see, many of these issues were subsequently sidelined as the central government began to formulate a strategy to prevent future disturbances.

The reports into the disturbances were crucial in setting the stage for a sustained critique of multiculturalism once the backlash against it started. Therefore, it is important to examine them in more detail, and to see the evolution of government policies and public thinking as they digested, interpreted, and re-worked the findings and recommendations of the reports into an assault on multiculturalism.

All the reports pointed to the devastating impact of deindustrialization on employment levels and economic opportunities, with Asian levels of unemployment and poverty being particularly high, partly because the local authorities had few systematic policies for employing ethnic minorities. The loss of textile manufacturing partly contributed to the fact that all of the wards (districts) that were affected by the civil disturbances were among the 20% most deprived in the country, and some areas of Oldham and Burnley ranked amongst the poorest 1%. De-industrialization had led to shared deprivation amongst whites and Asians. The minority Asian communities had also faced sustained interpersonal racism from local whites, institutional racism from the governing urban councils which had discriminated against and segregated Asians in particular areas and types of housing (Oldham Council's housing policies had been condemned as racist by a Commission for Racial Equality investigation in the 1990s), and harassment from the Far-Right National Front. Local estate agents had often contributed to 'white flight' by panicking whites into moving out of areas as Asians started to buy houses there, stoking fears of falling house prices. Neighbourhoods and schools were thus becoming all-white or all-Asian.

The demise of local Racial Equality Councils meant that residents had nowhere to turn to for advice on discrimination, and there was no ongoing attempt at improving community relations. According to the reports, there was 'self-segregation' on the part of both communities, leading to a deep cultural divide between the Asians and the whites, with little interaction between them. In turn, this had led to ignorance and exaggerated fears about each other. Particularly, there were also continual, damaging myths about either Asians or whites – usually the former – getting an unfair share of local government resources. These myths were often the result of a competitive bidding process in which communities were pitted against each other, with inevitable resentments.

The bidding process was area-based, reinforcing spatial divisions between communities that had developed due to settlement patterns stemming from earlier processes of migration into areas where employment and housing were available to incoming ethnic minorities, before the development of conceptions of multiculturalism. The reports point out that the situation was made worse by the local media which tended to give unfair prominence to funds allocated to Asian areas while downplaying those provided for majority white areas, selective reporting that gave ammunition to the National Front in building up further resentment and hostility amongst white residents. The police were mistrusted as unfair, especially by Asians, but also whites who felt that Asians were allowed to get away with misdemeanours because Race Relations legislation shackled the police. The reports suggested that the police, often in collusion with local media, often exacerbated tensions by highlighting attacks by Asians on whites while underplaying violence and routine harassment against Asians (for example, the throwing of rubbish into Asian backyards which was widespread).

According to the reports, the actual disturbances, taking place against this background, were provoked by a range of local incidents such as violence against an Asian taxi driver, rumours of imminent incursions or actual marches by the National Front in Asian areas, alleged turf wars amongst rival white and Asian gangs involved in dealing drugs, and so forth. Inevitably, the participants in the disorders were young men from the Pakistani, Bangladeshi, and white communities, although the obvious role of forms of masculinity in fomenting violence went completely unremarked in the reports.

While the reports were thus obviously aware of the multi-causality surrounding the events and advised more research and investigation, they identified the main underlying issue as being the fracturing of local communities with the result that Asians and whites were now leading what the Cantle Report called 'parallel

4. Young British Asians protesting on the streets

lives', with little intercommunal dialogue and much intercommunal hostility which had been left to fester by lack of adequate local leadership from the councils and community leaders.

Inadequate levels of competence in English, especially amongst new brides and the older generation, were remarked upon as barriers, but young Asian women were also praised in the Oldham and Bradford Reports for leading projects that involved intercommunal interaction and sharing of experiences.

'Multiculturalism' did not cause segregation and riots: it's official

The civil disturbances of summer 2001 have always been cited as evidence that multiculturalism in Britain had failed, a judgement reinforced by the involvement of British South Asian Muslims in terrorist bombings in London in July 2005.

72

Contrary to the impression that is now embedded in the public imagination and government policies that the official reports into the 2001 disorders concurred with this judgement, quite the opposite is the case. A close reading of the reports suggests that the case subsequently mounted against multiculturalism has to be reappraised.

Multiculturalism in fact gets hardly any mention in the Reports on Oldham and Burnley. One direct use of the term is in the Burnley Report where the *absence* of 'multicultural activities' is lamented. What is really striking about the reports is their regret at the almost complete absence of multiculturalism and their call for more of it. This is especially in education, but also in local authority practices, media reporting, employment practices, and leisure facilities.

The Bradford Race Review team explicitly criticized the National Curriculum, which had been created by the pre-1997 Conservative administrations as a deliberate strategy to sideline multiculturalist initiatives in schools, for failing to teach about 'different cultures and faiths among our diverse multi-cultural communities'. The team cited evidence from their discussions that young people considered this a particular deficiency in their education.

The Oldham Report wanted much greater effort to be put into a 'celebration of the town's diversity' and the way in which 'different groups of immigrants have enriched and contributed to the socio-economic life of Oldham'. It also argued that 'respect' needed to be instilled into Oldham's residents 'for others' traditions and viewpoints', combined with 'greater education in cultural awareness', and 'a willingness to listen to the other person's point of view'. These are urgent demands for more multiculturalism, involving a valuing of cultural diversity, a recognition of the contribution of immigrants, and developing empathy between different ethnic communities.

Given the key role played by the diagnosis of cities composed of fractured communities, it is not surprising that all the reports recommend more mixing, to rectify embedded patterns of residential and educational segregation. *But multiculturalism is not blamed for the creation of segregation and fractured communities.*

The idea of 'self'-segregation by each community, Asian and white, is also a strong motif. The reports also emphasized that there were people in all the communities who were keen on more intercommunal interaction and mixing. There is, of course, independent evidence, especially from journalistic accounts like that of Kenan Malik, that faith-based funding, demanded by community groups, did further entrench divisions that already existed on the ground in Bradford, Birmingham, and other cities. But more systematic research by Farrar and by Solomos and Back also reveals a more complex picture of processes of political negotiation and mobilization than can be captured by any simplistic blaming of 'multiculturalism' for communal divisions.

Moreover, a reading of the findings of the reports reveals that racism amongst the white population, combined with discrimination in housing allocation by the councils, racism amongst employers, the activities of estate agents, and selective anti-Asian local media reporting played a much larger role in creating segregation than Asian resistance to integration and cultural preference for living within the narrow confines of their own neighbourhoods. And much of the desire to interact and mix came from the Asians rather than the whites.

The Oldham panel was 'shocked' by the racism it found amongst the whites and recommended 'the need to tackle racism and racist attitudes...as a matter of the utmost urgency'. And on resistance to mixing: 'Attempts at mixing Asian and white families in Council properties have been largely unsuccessful, *because of racist victimization of incoming Asian families*' (my emphasis).

The Bradford Report also emphasizes that the inner-city white population did not appear to accept that Muslims had any place in the city and had distanced itself from 'the Bradford identity'. The report also expressed significant concerns over racial discrimination in employment.

'Sleepwalking into segregation': does Britain have ghettos and are they produced by multiculturalism?

None of the reports into the 2001 disturbances blame multiculturalism for the events or the underlying social factors that had led to divisions and hostility between communities. And they certainly do not use the term 'ghetto' to describe the ethnic 'clustering' they were told about by residents of the cities. Equally striking is the admission in the reports that as yet there were no measures of the degree of segregation that existed in the 'mill towns'. Therefore they called for more systematic and rigorous research to establish to what extent the segregation between the communities was a real phenomenon.

That the fear of ethnic 'ghettos' gripped the nation, especially as a cause of dangerous alienation amongst young Muslims, is something partly owed to Trevor Phillips, then chairman of the Commission for Racial Equality, in a well-publicized speech and other remarks in the wake of the July 2005 bombings in London perpetrated by several young Asian men. Britain, he warned, was in danger of 'sleepwalking' its way into segregation and 'some districts are on their way to becoming fully fledged ghettos – black holes into which no-one goes without fear and trepidation'. And he linked this specifically to the dangers of home-grown Islamic terrorism: 'The aftermath of 7/7 forces us to assess where we are . . . We are becoming strangers to each other.' He talked of 'marooned communities' whose members would increasingly regard 'the codes of behaviour, loyalty and respect that the rest of us take for granted as outdated'. This was his ominous conclusion: 'We know what follows then: crime, no-go areas and chronic cultural conflict.' And multiculturalism, he said, had to accept a large share of the blame, for

> in recent years we have focused far too much on the 'multi' and not enough on common culture. We've emphasized what divides us ... We have allowed tolerance of diversity to harden into effective isolation of communities, in which some people think special separate values ought to apply.

Multiculturalism, segregation, violence, and terrorism were already becoming linked in the public imagination as the Right-wing media especially had started this chain of association and gained extra ammunition from Phillips's comments. In *The Daily Telegraph*, Mark Steyn had already presaged Phillips's conclusion by claiming that 'The real suicide bomb is "multiculturalism" ' (19 July 2005).

However, the 2001 Reports had already inspired serious investigation by urban geographers, demographers, and sociologists at British universities: for example, Deborah Phillips at Leeds, Ceri Peach at Oxford, Ludi Simpson and Nissa Finney at Manchester, and others, most of whom had also been researching these issues well before the disorders.

Almost all the key assertions in the 2001 Reports about 'segregation', repeated in other government reports and policy documents, and thus the supposed evidence underlying the subsequent attacks on multiculturalism, have turned out to be myths according to a systematic synthesis by Finney and Simpson. Here are just some of their relevant conclusions derived from their own and other research evidence:

- There are no ghettos in Britain and the population movements are producing more diversity in local areas not less. Britain is not 'sleepwalking into segregation'. Bradford, about which the first of the fears of segregation was expressed, is typical of the rest of the country where South Asian, Caribbean, and other migrants have settled. Even in the most Asian areas, more than 25% of residents are white.

- While there has been growth of the minority population in minority-dominated wards, this is from natural growth rather than new immigration.

- Minority residents are moving out of the wards where they predominated, into other parts of the UK: more minority residents are moving out than moving in. The arrival of Eastern European and African migrants is making areas more diverse as Asian dominance is declining.

- Considered in a longer time frame, 'white flight' is also a myth. White residents have been moving into minority concentrations in Leicester, Bradford, Lambeth, Wolverhampton, Manchester, and elsewhere, while ethnic minority residents have been moving out. Moreover, in general, all groups over time are moving out of depressed industrial cities to jobs or better housing elsewhere.

- The highest ethnic concentration is for whites, which is not surprising given that six out of every seven residents in Britain is white. The average white person lives in a ward with 90% white people in it; in contrast, the average Pakistani in Britain lives in a ward containing 17% Pakistanis.

- The proportion of Muslims charged with terrorism offences is not higher in areas where there are many Muslims compared to areas that have few. So the notion that radicalized Muslims are isolated and tend to live and study with other Muslims is not true.

- While many schools have significant ethnic minority populations, most of these schools are, of course, predominantly white simply because whites make up the majority of the population. There is no evidence that school choice is increasing segregation. While there has been an increase in ethnic segregation in some areas, this is accounted for by an increase in the ethnic minority population. There has been a greater increase in segregation by income than by ethnicity.

- Moreover, research shows that ethnic minority parents express a preference for their children to enrol in ethnically mixed schools. And Asian young women are particularly keen that their children should grow up in mixed areas; to try and ensure this, they tend to buy houses in the suburbs.
- The available evidence contradicts the widely held view that the friendship groups of young people are increasingly restricted to single ethnic groups. In particular, there is increased mixing of friendship groups amongst British-born ethnic minorities.
- One of the fastest-growing ethnic minorities is the 'Mixed' group, showing a particular tendency amongst British citizens of different ethnicities to intermarry. Strikingly, Asian Muslims, Sikhs, and Hindus are marrying out of their own groups as often as are white Christians.
- As the 2001 reports suggested, and this is confirmed by opinion polls, in general it is whites who are less likely to want to actually engage, mix, and 'integrate' with ethnic minorities than the other way around. Thus the call for greater emphasis on celebrating diversity.
- A key Finney and Simpson conclusion is that 'An assimilationist agenda placing responsibility for integration exclusively on the shoulders of minorities is clearly not a viable option', although this is exactly the thrust of most recent government initiatives (of which more later).

The evidence appears to challenge the idea of growing ethnic segregation in British cities. Blaming multiculturalism for something that has not actually been occurring obviously makes no sense at all.

However, some aspects of Finney and Simpson's findings have been challenged by Carling and also by Phillips. The former points out that we should not completely discount the notion of self-segregation amongst the Pakistani-origin South Asian communities of Bradford, motivated by a desire to retain links and take advantage of the opportunities for mosque attendance, shopping, kin networks, and so forth, and to some degree this process will continue. And also that 'white flight' is a real process, albeit mixed with middle-class aspiration as well as a desire to get away from 'immigrants'. Deborah Phillips has shown that there is middle-class Asian flight, with larger numbers moving out to the suburbs; also, Sikhs, Hindus, and Muslims often move to different areas, creating separate suburban enclaves, although there is no evidence that multiculturalism has anything to do with these processes of differentiation.

Thus separation between South Asians and whites is a continuing issue whether ghettos technically exist or not. We have little information on the quality of the relationships between the communities. Even when they live in close proximity, we do not know what degree of interaction, neighbourliness, and 'conviviality' – a term that has gained some currency recently – exists and to what degree grudging co-existence is the norm, ready to turn into confrontation under real or imagined provocation.

On a more positive note, Carling points to many initiatives that are currently active in Bradford which bring the different communities together in a constructive manner, some of which I shall discuss in the next chapter.

Simpson and Finney's favoured policies consist of addressing questions of housing and employment opportunities amongst all communities, on the assumption that alleviating material deprivation is above all what matters.

In so far as this is the case, Simpson and Finney could be accused of being surprisingly naive. The relationship between material deprivation and racism is a complex one; there is no one-to-one correlation between the two, and Carling also points out that in Bradford many of the voters for the openly racist BNP come from affluent areas.

While many of Simpson and Finney's arguments have considerable force, they appear to underestimate the degree to which policies are needed to tackle issues relating to ethnic relations as ethnic relations rather than simply as matters of inequality and material deprivation. It is all too easy to dismiss such considerations as 'merely cultural', but they will not go away solely by improving life chances in all communities, extremely desirable though that is.

Whatever the number of caveats entered, the 2001 reports and evidence before and since suggest that we now confront a situation in Britain in which on average the white population in particular has little understanding of the beliefs and lifestyles of ethnic minorities, is easily susceptible to myths propagated in popular media and by the Far Right, and actually remains more unwilling to mix and engage with ethnic minorities. There are likely to be myths about the white population in circulation amongst ethnic minorities, but living in British society, going through a British education, engaging with British popular culture, and developing hybrid, complex, syncretic, multiple, hyphenated identities means, as we shall see, that there is far less likelihood of a simplistic, ignorant rejection of all things 'white British'. White British identities are also being transformed, especially amongst the young, and this undoubtedly means that any new initiatives in 'multiculturalism' in the broadest sense will have to take account of forms of cultural diversity that are significantly different from the 1990s.

And as we will see in the next chapter, social class segregation, gated communities, and the stalling of social mobility are important factors affecting the cohesion of local communities.

Before confronting the difficult questions surrounding the future of multiculturalism, though, we need to pay attention to what has been happening to multiculturalism in mainland Europe.

Multiculturalism in comparative perspective: lessons from France and the Netherlands

By the late 1990s, some in France, principally amongst the intellectuals, had begun to ask for a rethinking of the country's dominant assimilationist model of 'integrating' immigrants, one which actually refused all recognition of cultural claims and thus did not accept the existence of 'ethnic minorities'. Alan Touraine was one amongst a small but growing number who argued that the French needed to borrow some elements from British and North American multiculturalism.

But Britain's 2001 disorders soon appeared to make such demands look misguided, to say the least. They were widely seen in France as evidence that 'Anglo-Saxon' multiculturalism was a dismal failure and that France's integrationism was a far superior mode of incorporating non-European immigrants. 9/11 and Britain's 7/7 (2005) were further nails in the coffin of multiculturalist demands in France, as even the British began to panic about lack of 'social cohesion' and started furiously backpedalling on previous commitments to cultural pluralism.

French complacency, however, was soon punctured by the events of the autumn of 2005 as the suburbs, or *banlieues*, of Paris and well over 250 other towns, or *communes*, experienced serious rioting by mostly immigrant-origin youth. And nor was this the first time. Between 1981 and 2003, French towns had witnessed smaller or larger disorders of this kind on over a dozen occasions. Resentment against police harassment or confrontations with the police were usually the triggers and led to nights of car-burning and attacks on official buildings, which in 2005 included schools, sports halls, and municipal buildings, giving an indication of the hostility felt towards official French institutions. These were France's worst disorders since the famous events of May 1968.

Those who had smugly blamed multiculturalism for disorders in British cities found themselves confronting a serious dilemma. France, as we have seen, did not officially have 'ethnic minorities' and had never officially adopted multicultural policies. Public debates hardly ever explicitly talked about race or ethnic relations or racism. French public discourse simply referred to 'urban problems'. Yet the main participants in the disorders were clearly very aggrieved French-born youth of North African and sub-Saharan African origin, just as Britain's disturbances had largely involved ethnic minority youth (with provocation from and fights with Far-Right white youth).

While the French state had always eschewed collecting statistics based on ethnicity, and there was no official monitoring of discrimination against non-European-origin immigrants and their offspring, sociologists and others, alerted especially by a series of disturbances throughout the 1990s, had been steadily conducting research into just such issues. In the aftermath of autumn 2005 – and further disturbances in 2007 and 2009 – much more of the relevant information is now in the public domain.

Nicolas Sarkozy, while Interior Minister in 2005, had dismissed the youth from the suburban housing estates as scum (*racaille*) and saw the disruptions simply as criminal behaviour. In stark contrast, even the French domestic intelligence service blamed the disorders on social inequality and exclusion.

Since the 1980s, the de-industrialization that affected all the Western European towns, including Britain's 'mill towns', had also taken a heavy toll in France's industrial centres, with immigrants and their children bearing a heavy burden of unemployment and deteriorating housing conditions and urban facilities in the outer suburbs. Unemployment rates amongst youth of North African origin had begun to rise alarmingly. As Alec Hargreaves has pointed out, a pioneering survey in the early 1990s

(Geographical Mobility and Social Incorporation – MGIS) had already discovered that the rate of unemployment amongst second-generation ethnic Algerians aged between 20 and 29 was a staggering 42% for men and 40% for women. And throughout the 1990s, unemployment in what were called the *Zones Urbaines Sensibles* (ZUS), where ethnic minorities are over-represented, rose even higher. In 2004, in a study to test employment discrimination, University of Paris researchers sent out *résumés* from fictitious job applicants to more than 200 French employers. A *résumé* with a classic French name received more than five time as many positive responses as one with a North African name, although both listed identical qualifications. As Hargreaves puts it:

> For well over a decade, youth unemployment among visible minorities had been so high that many young people of Maghrebi [North African], sub-Saharan African and Caribbean origin had come to despair of ever finding regular employment.

Combined with anger at discrimination, their frustration had boiled over on a number of occasions, but most spectacularly in the autumn of 2005.

The non-European immigrant-origin youth were not questioning the French integration or assimilationist Republican model of citizenship. All the interviews with them conducted by sociologists and cited by Duprez, Hargreaves, Muchielli, and others confirmed that what they were demanding was a fulfilment of the promises of equal treatment promised in the French idea of citizenship but which they were being denied by blatant discrimination in the labour market and provocative police harassment. The youth involved were not militant multiculturalists or Islamicist *jihadists* angered by non-recognition of their cultural identities. Indeed, research on these French young people has consistently confirmed that they identify themselves as French, first and foremost, with little allegiance to the countries from which their parents and grandparents had migrated (only a small proportion of those of North African origin actually speak Arabic, although public and everyday discourse refers to them as 'Arabs' and refuses to acknowledge their Frenchness). And they were certainly not mindless criminals bent on senseless destruction. Many were the graduates who suffer twice the level of unemployment as those with typically French European names, revealed in the Paris study.

The Sarkozy jibe of 'scum' and his threat to 'cleanse the estates with pressure washers' were thus particularly insulting and provocative. Equally misguided has been the French state's policy response, which has been to toughen the already oppressive policing – abandoning the experiments in community policing (*police de proximité*) pioneered earlier – and the introduction of even tighter immigration rules, which had already begun in the 1980s and 1990s, partly as a response to the gains of the virulently anti-immigrant *Front National*.

In a move that has echoes elsewhere in Europe, President Sarkozy has introduced new 'integration' laws, including a 'Welcome and Integration Contract' for immigrants which demands that they uphold the 'laws and values of France' and attend language and civic courses. Given the level of cultural integration already achieved by those in the *banlieues*, these new regulations, much like the similar ones in the UK, seem to be particularly inappropriate.

However, the French have also begun to make tentative moves in a more multiculturalist direction, although the term remains taboo in French public discourse. Demands by sociologists and other researchers in the 1990s for official statistics on ethnic minorities and forms of ethnic monitoring to track discrimination against 'visible minorities' were given added impetus by the 1998 report of the *Haut Conseil à l'Intégration* (HCI), which actually recommended the setting up of a state-funded agency along the lines of the British Commission for Racial Equality (CRE) that could investigate cases of racial discrimination. The EU directive of 2000 demanding of all member states that they set up independent anti-discriminatory bodies has led to the establishment of the *Haute autorité de lutte contre les discriminations et pour l'égalité* (HALDE), but which has powers and resources that are considerably less than the (now defunct) CRE.

Hargreaves' judgement on recent French initiatives, though, is damning. For all the new public discourses on 'diversity' and 'equal opportunity' that have now replaced the discredited talk of 'integration', he says:

> At every step in the incremental changes seen since 1997, the anti-discrimination initiatives taken by governments of both left and the centre-right have been half baked and some would say half-hearted.

The fact that the department of national statistics has in November 2010 officially published figures showing higher unemployment rates for French citizens with parents from the Maghreb, and its admission that discrimination appears to have played a major role in the disadvantage suffered by those of immigrant origin, is potentially an important development whose impact on future policies is as yet unclear.

Nevertheless, it is significant that the French have had to move away from simplistic notions of integration to the recognition of diversity and equal opportunity as important public objectives. The Ministry of Immigration and National Identity was abolished in November 2010 after only a short life. 'Multiculturalism-lite', perhaps, but a definite shift away from the previously militant opposition to 'Anglo-Saxon' social models in relation to ethnic minorities and their place in French social institutions.

Neither the 2001 'mill town' disturbances nor the hesitant but definite French moves towards the recognition of 'cultural diversity', 'equal opportunities', and even ethnic monitoring suggest that it is multiculturalism that is to blame for social disintegration. And the extent of social disintegration has been grossly exaggerated in both countries. The truth appears to be that some aspects of multiculturalism may provide a more appropriate response than simple calls for more 'integration'.

However, the Dutch retreat from multiculturalism suggests that there might still be a case for multiculturalism to answer as a harbinger of social disintegration.

As we have seen in the first chapter, Dutch multiculturalism, although never referred to as such, emerged as 'Minorities Policy' in the 1980s, following nearly two decades in which a combination of the Dutch pillarization model and the expectation that non-European immigrants especially were only 'guest workers' destined to return 'home' after a relatively short period produced a system that almost encouraged a cultural ghettoization in which the immigrants had their own-language newspapers, radio and television broadcasts, and the teaching of mother tongues in schools.

Although in some ways the move from guest worker to multicultural policies is easier than a shift from assimilation priorities because a culturally pluralist infrastructure is already in place, nevertheless it is also arguable that the peculiarity of the Dutch case also hampered multiculturalism. That is, in so far as multiculturalism involves a celebration of diversity, a greater or lesser change in a nation's historical sense of itself informed by a general orientation towards integration and a commitment to equal opportunities via anti-discrimination, the Dutch approach where the immigrant minorities had been strongly encouraged to identify with their homeland – which would not happen in an assimilationist or conventional multiculturalist model – entrenches within the minority and the majority a strong sense that the minorities do not belong and should not attempt to belong.

This positive encouragement of non-belonging obviously also meant that too little groundwork had been done in developing anti-discriminatory cultures and policies amongst public and private employers, in social services, in education, and in leisure facilities.

It was only in 1994 that UK-style anti-discrimination legislation was introduced, with the Law on Equal Treatment. By then, a significant 1989 Report from the Scientific Council for Government had raised the alarm about very high levels of unemployment and low levels of educational achievement amongst minorities of non-European immigrant origin: Turkish- and Moroccan-origin minorities had an unemployment rate of 30% compared with 6% amongst workers of Dutch origin. As in the rest of Western Europe, the low-skilled jobs for which the immigrant workers had been recruited were fast disappearing.

The official 'Minorities Policy', the Dutch version of multiculturalism, gave way to an explicit 'Integration Policy'. By 1997, Dutch language and civic integration courses became mandatory for newcomers, an initiative that was to be widely borrowed by other European states. The move was prompted by a new debate about a possible clash between liberal Dutch values and what were thought to be non-liberal, repressive Islamic values. Curiously, the debates were provoked not by events in the Netherlands, but the Rushdie affair in Britain and the headscarf controversy in France. Research carried out by Paul Sniderman and Louk Hagendoorn in 1997, although only published in 2007, seemed to confirm widespread anxiety about Islamic values amongst the Dutch, although the study was deeply flawed: the way the questionnaires were designed encouraged respondents to think in polarized terms, pitting 'Muslim' and 'Islamic' values against 'Western European' values in a crude, homogenizing manner. The 1990s debates soon died down because of the absence of a specific Dutch resonance at the time, although arguably the seeds had been sown for a full-scale assault on the failure of Dutch multiculturalism. In the 1990s, despite the end of the guest-worker regime, the fact that so many people of Turkish and Moroccan origin continued to have a strong identification with their countries of origin was regarded as evidence of the *success* of the Dutch model of encouraging cultural preservation.

But the immigrant-origin minorities were also changing. Research by sociologists such as Han Entzinger and others carried out in Rotterdam, published in 2000, revealed that youth of Moroccan and Turkish origin were developing their own Westernized versions of Islam. They strongly supported principles such as individual freedom and equality. And as Entzinger has pointed out, he and his co-researchers discovered that 'as their educational level goes up, their ideas became more liberal and differences with Dutch young people of the same educational background virtually disappear'.

But a different narrative had begun to circulate amongst sections of the Dutch political and intellectual elite. This was one of the emergence of a Dutch underclass of immigrant-minority origin, alienated from Dutch society and culture and unwilling to integrate. It revived the earlier fear of a 'civilizational' conflict between the Dutch and their non-European minorities of Muslim origin. The events of 9/11 led to a huge leap in anti-immigration sentiment, fed by the Dutch media and expertly exploited by Pim Fortuyn, whose anti-immigrant party had considerable success in the 2002 parliamentary elections and entered a coalition government.

A new anti-immigrant discourse took shape and gained influence. Although Fortuyn's assassination by an animal rights activist eventually led to a decline in his party's fortunes, his fears of a widespread anti-democratic, and especially homophobic and women-subordinating, culture became firmly established in new Dutch policies towards immigrants and their descendants. The assassination of the film-maker Theo van Gogh by a 26-year-old of Moroccan origin after the broadcast of *Submission*, which he had helped to make with the Dutch MP of Somali origin Ayaan Hirshi Ali, and which featured verses of the Qur'an projected upon a naked, veiled woman to highlight the view that the Qur'an promotes violence against women, only seemed to confirm fears about Muslims and Islam as a threat to liberal Dutch culture.

Acquiring Dutch citizenship, as I have pointed out in the first chapter, has become increasingly costly and difficult. The 'integration' courses now have to be paid for, a test has to be taken within five years of settlement in the Netherlands, and fines are imposed for failing the test. Proposals have been made for 'oldcomers' who are already settled to take courses and tests, with fines as penalties for failure. As in other European countries, which have often taken their cue from the Dutch, immigrants now have to demonstrate commitment to 'Dutch values and norms'.

What, then, are the lessons of multiculturalism as instituted in the Netherlands? In the Netherlands, Britain, and elsewhere in Western Europe, the answer has seemed to be obvious: not only has Dutch multiculturalism been a failure, but multiculturalism in general has been shown to be obviously flawed. The Dutch retreat from multiculturalism is in fact seen as especially significant, given that the Netherlands had been viewed as a place that had been perhaps the most enthusiastic in its conception and implementation of multicultural policies.

But while there is some merit in this interpretation, it is important to have a rather more nuanced view. Let us begin with Entzinger's wry judgement on the Dutch case: as he puts it, we have 'the paradox that migrants who initially had been encouraged to preserve their own identity were now blamed for insufficiently identifying with Dutch culture'. Entzinger's point is important, for the more multicultural 'Minorities Policy' of the 1980s and 1990s had come after a long period of pillarization in which minorities had been deliberately kept at arm's length from Dutch culture and had been publicly subsidized and positively encouraged not to regard the Netherlands as 'home'. Belated attempts at a genuinely multicultural form of integration, including therefore a national celebration of cultural diversity, had to cut against the grain of a long-established national view of immigrant minorities as having no long-term place in Dutch society and culture.

Moreover, the late adoption of serious anti-discriminatory policies meant that the socio-economic marginalization of non-European immigrants and their offspring had also become strongly entrenched and was difficult to turn around. It is perverse to blame multiculturalism for the emergence of an immigrant-origin 'underclass' when the equal opportunities, let alone anti-racist, part of the multicultural settlement had come so late.

The life history of Mohammed B., the murderer of Theo van Gogh, became something of a test case in Dutch debates about multiculturalism. For many, he embodied the failure of Dutch multiculturalism: a high-school dropout who came to embrace radical Islam. But Mohammed B.'s story turns out to be more complex and ambiguous. Born in the Netherlands, he had done well at secondary school, had studied accountancy and social work, and was an active volunteer social worker in a youth work programme in his part of Amsterdam. As Anna Korteweg has pointed out, after studying Mohammed's life in some detail, Mohammed's work entailed encouraging other Moroccan-origin youth to continue their education despite the fact that he had not himself finished his post-secondary school studies.

And the idea that Mohammed B. is a dramatic example of the failure of multiculturalism is countered by the Dutch sociologist Ewald Engelen. Mohammed B. was a volunteer worker. In effect, he was unemployed and received social security payments. For Engelen, Mohammed B.'s fate is a typical example of a flawed and *incomplete* multiculturalism, a strategy which gave group cultural rights 'but in the absence of an effective anti-discrimination policy in the sphere of labour market insertion'. Indeed, his conclusion is that

> the case of Mohammed B. does not so much demonstrate that
> Dutch multiculturalism had gone too far...but rather that
> there was not *enough* multiculturalism in the Netherlands. The
> lesson could just as well be that the combination of enforced
> assimilation, as is the course the Dutch have taken since the rise
> and fall of Pim Fortuyn in 2002, and malign neglect in the socio-
> economic sphere are a sure recipe for Islamic radicalization.
> (emphasis in original)

Indeed, the lesson from both France and the Netherlands is that no simple narrative of the wholesale failure of 'multiculturalism' can be sustained. The French have been moving slowly but more or less steadily towards a version of it, especially at a local level. And there are enough students of the Dutch case who argue that there has been a public over-reaction into militant forms of assimilation when a more successful strategy would be a recalibration of the peculiar Dutch model of pillarizaton into which the nation's multiculturalism was shoe-horned.

But there are other more general conclusions one might draw. For one thing, the hasty rhetoric of retreat from multiculturalism in the UK and elsewhere in Western Europe arguably suffers from the same flaw that has been identified for the Netherlands by Engelen. The Reports into the 2001 English disturbances after all argued in effect that there had not been enough multiculturalism. And detailed accounts of other cities,

Birmingham for example, researched by Solomos and Back, show how in the 1990s there had actually been a retreat from equal opportunity policies and thus a failure to tackle urban racial disadvantage.

Re-reading riot(ous) acts: official interpretations of the events of 2001 (UK) and 2005 (France) and the backlash against multiculturalism

It is clear from all accounts of the 'mill town' disturbances of 2001 in England and the 2005 events in the French *banlieues* that the ethnic minority youth involved were not asking for group cultural rights or the preservation of 'traditions' from their parents' homelands. They were actually demanding full inclusion in the British and French nation states as citizens with equal opportunities and rights to participate in and contribute to the nation.

In the case of the 'mill town' events, incursions by the Far-Right British National Party posed real threats to the safety and integrity of the South Asian communities. The detailed study by Paul Bagguley and Yasmin Hussein into the disturbances in Bradford graphically reveal the degree to which the youth of Pakistani origin felt genuinely and legitimately threatened by BNP marches and damage to their properties and persons.

But as Bagguley and Hussein also point out, the 2001 reports were ambivalently framed. They could therefore be read in such a way that the blame for the disturbances could be laid squarely on certain characteristics of the ethnic minorities themselves. That is, elements of the reports *pathologized* the South Asian communities and allowed the government to argue that the main changes had to happen within these communities, and in the multicultural policies that had supposedly allowed them for too long to segregate themselves and develop dysfunctional social habits without adequate supervision and pressure from local and central authorities.

In particular, the reports tended to simply list a variety of causal factors without being able to give weighting, for example, to de-industrialization, unemployment, and racial discrimination in housing and employment, as opposed to a desire to live amongst themselves, in creating segregation, and for which in any case no measure was provided. This meant that in its official response to the events and the reports, the government was able to cherry-pick supposed causes of the 'riots' and to frame policy options on the basis of its own preferred agenda.

And this is how the 2001 events became part of a drive to abandon multiculturalism, to engender 'integration' and 'community cohesion' instead, and to marginalize issues of socio-economic deprivation and racism from the Far-Right and in local policies in blighting the lives of the minorities.

In France, the Netherlands, and elsewhere, the ideas of integration and common values to unite minorities and the majorities have also come to form the centrepiece of new citizenship policies. However, in France, as I have noted in Chapter 1, President Sarkozy has now abolished the widely criticized ministry for immigration and national identity. But 'integration' remains a dominant theme in the new alternatives to multiculturalism, and it is time now to assess their appropriateness to the issues facing multiethnic European nation states in the present.

Chapter 4

'Integration', class inequality, and 'community cohesion'

As the backlash against multiculturalism has gathered pace, it has been replaced by 'integration' as the key theme of national and local policies towards ethnic minorities throughout Europe. In addition, especially in the UK, the ideas of 'community cohesion', 'social cohesion', and 'citizenship' have also been heavily trailed as the new way forward in managing the incorporation of ethnic minorities into the national polity. The British government now has communities ministers, a Commission for Integration and Cohesion, and new government departments. And throughout Western Europe, there has been a new emphasis on clarifying the meaning of 'national identity' so as to better integrate ethnic minorities into national cultures. In all but name, cynics might want to argue, a new European civilizing mission appears to have been launched.

But the meaning of these ideas and the policies that flow from them have inevitably proved contentious. Nor is it the case that supporters of multiculturalism have just faded away. A lively debate is under way, although sometimes it may seem as if the only defenders of multiculturalism now are to be found in academia and a few activist and ethnic minority strongholds.

The pitfalls of 'integration'

The idea that the key problem in ethnic relations is a failure on the part of minorities to 'integrate' into the European societies into which they have migrated is a central motif of the new approach that is replacing multiculturalism. However, as we have seen, there appears to be no clear line linking multiculturalist policies with civil disturbances, terrorism, or suicide bombings. Moreover, the evidence on the degree of separation and segregation is contentious, at least in Britain. And even in the Netherlands and France, together with Britain, it is the incomplete and half-hearted character of multiculturalism that has been highlighted, equally plausibly, by many well-informed researchers and commentators as the real problem.

In social life, it is never clear what counts as complete integration nor who can be said to be fully integrated. Goalposts can be moved at will. In the 1980s in Britain, the Conservative politician Norman Tebbit devised the cricket test: minorities could not claim to be integrated until they supported England rather than India, Pakistan, or the West Indies in England's cricket matches with these countries. Early in the 21st century, the New Labour Home Secretary David Blunkett decided that the speaking of English in the home by minorities was the route to integration as well as one key index.

So, one might well ask: integration into exactly what? One answer that many European governments have come up with incorporates the idea of core national values, labelled 'Britishness' or French national identity, for example. However, as we shall see, this type of thinking runs into some intractable problems.

Social scientists have been arguing for a very long time that integration when applied to social life, and immigration processes in particular, is a multidimensional concept. There is no single measure of the process. Integration can take place at spatial levels (for example, residential patterns), structural levels (for example, in education and the labour market), and cultural levels (for example, in adherence to common values). Moreover, there is no necessary relation between the three, so that neighbours can subscribe to very different values, and high educational and occupational achievements can occur despite spatial separation, and so forth.

The UK government was warned of the extraordinary complexity and multidimensionality of processes of integration soon after the 2001 disorders in a document by the Oxford University research centres, for Migration and Policy, and Refugee Studies, which were commissioned by the UK Home Office to provide an advisory report on the subject, *Integration: Mapping the Field* (2002).

The rise and rise of 'community cohesion'

In Britain, the concept of integration was soon eclipsed by the overlapping but distinct discourse of 'community cohesion', which had made its appearance in British debates at more or less the same time, being mentioned in the Cantle and Denham Reports initiated by the UK Home Office (2001, 2002); the Denham Report was explicitly entitled *Building Cohesive Communities*.

This change moved the agenda even further away from commitment to multiculturalism; echoes of earlier demands for immigrants to assimilate seemed to be surfacing as well. And it began to compete with important measures such as the Human Rights Act (1998), the emphasis on combating institutional racism as recommended by the Macpherson Report on policing after the police failures revealed in the aftermath of the black teenager Stephen Lawrence's murder, and the Race Relations Amendment Act (2000).

'Community cohesion' occupied centre stage in UK Government policies in the wake of the events of 2001. I shall examine the three key sources of the notion of community cohesion, noting some of the criticisms that each strand has attracted, before examining the idea as a whole and the policies to which it has given rise.

The sources of 'community cohesion'

1. Communitarianism

Communitarianism had emerged in the 1990s as a sort of 'third way' perspective, critical of both the new Right and the Left for dissolving the 'social glue' that had held locales and society as a whole together. The former was blamed for the excesses of free-market individualism and libertarianism which had helped erode ethics of social responsibility and norms of reciprocity, epitomized in Mrs Thatcher's notorious 'there is no such thing as society' nostrum. The Left was castigated for too much bureaucratized centralization which had drained power away from local communities, together with welfare systems that failed to properly support independent social networks and did little to help the institution of the family.

However, as sociologists and anthropologists have pointed out time and again, the concept of community is surprisingly nebulous. It is very difficult to define with any precision. When does a social group constitute a genuine 'community'? How much unity should it display and in what characteristics? The question of whether Internet networks constitute 'communities' highlights well the difficulties involved. The question of when a community is a community replicates the problems involved in deciding when a group is really integrated with another or within itself. When the two ideas are used together, as in the notion of 'integrated communities', which is intrinsic to the concept of community cohesion, the difficulties are compounded. There is here, too, a link with the problem of essentialism discussed earlier. It is too easy to make the assumption that communities are homogeneous and strongly bounded.

It has also been argued that the discourse of 'community' has allowed issues to be de-racialized, so that racism is not mentioned, and minority communities are pathologized as not living properly 'British' lives without also acknowledging that language-learning facilities are often hard to access and thinly available, but also that second- and third-generation minority women are increasingly successful in education and the professions and that racial discrimination and harassment are important reasons why minority groups continue to stay together in original areas of settlement.

'Community', in other words, is a bland enough notion, but in the case of 'community cohesion', it often conceals skewed and unfair descriptions of ethnic minority social groups.

2. The theory of 'social capital'

It was the publication in 2000 of the Harvard political scientist Robert Putnam's *Bowling Alone: The Collapse and Revival of American Community* that helped propel the already influential concept of social capital into serious global debate and allowed it to have an important impact on social policy in various parts of the world, especially through its adoption by international agencies such as the World Bank.

The notion of 'community' is central to this framework and dovetails well with communitarian thinking. This enables an easy insertion of the concept of social capital into the community cohesion agenda.

Putnam defines social capital as 'the connections among individuals – social networks and the norms of reciprocity and trustworthiness that arise from them'. He emphasizes that high social capital allows participants in the dense networks to trust each other and act together to pursue and achieve shared objectives. In principle, a distinction is made between 'bonding' and 'bridging' social capital. 'Bonding' capital is identified with cohesion *amongst* defined communities; it brings together people who are 'like one another', whether in relation to class, ethnicity, gender, or age. 'Bridging' capital is part of the process of the creation of overlapping networks *between* particular communities, bringing together people who are unlike each other. Putnam and his followers are aware that a high amount of bonding capital can have a 'dark' side, for it serves to create strong boundaries between insiders and 'others' who are thereby excluded and may be stigmatized. Thus bridging capital is a crucial component if wider social cohesion is to be achieved.

It is also in this context that the idea of *shared values* becomes important; too much cultural difference means less unity in values, and this is regarded as leading to low levels of bridging capital.

Putnam's narrative is one long lament for the disappearance of a once idyllic period in American history between the 1890s and the 1920s when the society was supposedly characterized by strong civic ties, high levels of civic and political participation, and high degrees of trust.

For the present malaise, as he sees it, he blames, contentiously, three developments: television, dual-career families, and urban sprawl. And his recommendation for reversing the decline of community in the USA is a new period of civic revival, with the development of community associations and civic and political participation, creating new forms of bonding and bridging social capital which can bind together a nation in danger of disastrously 'pulling apart'.

The attractions of this diagnosis and 'solution' to British policy-makers convinced that the crux of both the 'ethnic minority problem' and the wider social issues facing Britain is the fracturing of community relations should be obvious. Putnam gave seminars at 10 Downing Street. And the idea of building social capital in British cities became firmly embedded in government policies as an alternative to multiculturalism and the celebration and encouragement of 'diversity'.

Some of Putnam's work has focused on ethnic diversity, and he has concluded that ethnic diversity generally contributes to a decline in trust. There is, he argues, an urgent need to build bridging capital between diverse communities, and he recognizes too that this is more difficult than building the more inward-looking bonding capital. Citing Bosnia and Belfast, Putnam argues that bridging capital is vital for 'reconciling democracy and diversity'.

The wide influence of Putnam's version of the social capital thesis and the manner of its deployment in his historical and contemporary analyses belies its severe conceptual, methodological, and empirical limitations. And some of the limitations become particularly evident when more competent social research from the UK is considered, making the wholesale transfer of the Putnam thesis to the UK especially problematic and inappropriate.

Conceptually, social capital as he defines and uses it appears in the guise of a neutral, functional idea that serves to highlight issues of trust and reciprocity that are socially beneficial. But his usage ignores what many other sociologists have pointed out, that social capital also exists as 'cultural capital' which allows upper classes to build exclusive networks and a series of advantages, especially success in education, which enables a monopolization over generations of opportunities and access to other resources. Factor in the over-representation of ethnic minorities in the working classes in Europe, and to some extent – especially for African Americans – in the USA, and the conclusion is clear: social capital cannot simply be seen as a neutral resource for the benefit of the whole society.

There are two other peculiarities of the Putnam version of the social capital thesis. The emphasis is primarily on the quantity rather than the quality of relationships, such as friendliness and egalitarianism. Moreover, he takes a broad historical sweep, thus failing to deal with the historical specificity of locales and neighbourhoods and the traditions, social memories, and socio-economic and political inequalities that influence the quality of relationships between different social groups in different social spaces.

And Putnam's analysis ignores important social changes that have taken place, so that his indications and measures of bonding and bridging capital have become less and less relevant. As Barbara Arneil has shown, Putnam has continued to measure participation in conventional political parties and other traditional groups and institutions. This ignores the rise in alternative politics and looser forms of cultural participation – activities such as women's sport, women's political groups (women play a crucial role in Putnam's analysis without any acknowledgement of the way this skews his results and recommendations), and a whole range of ways in which individuals socialize and groups come together in late 20th-century America that are very different from the period that forms the base line for Putnam's comparison and lament of the decline of community.

Putnam's findings are not borne out when transferred, with greater conceptual and historical sophistication, to the British context. Peter Hall's analysis of British surveys reveals a different picture. For Britain, Hall concludes that there is little intergenerational difference in rates of participation in associations, and therefore little evidence of a decline in social capital. And in the case of women, there was a doubling of civic and political engagement in the period 1970 to 1990. One major reason for the different results is that Hall takes full account of the changes in women's educational experiences and achievements. As he shows, by 1990, 14% of British women had some post-secondary education, compared with hardly 1% in 1959. Putnam's analysis discounts the effects of changes in American women's education (a 12% increase in post-secondary educational experience), thus grossly underestimating increases in their participation rates and social capital. Hall's analysis suggests that the state and its educational policies have an important role to play in increasing civic and political engagement.

The difference in the types of associations that are included in Hall's survey compared with Putnam's is also important. Hall includes, for later periods, findings on participation in environmental movements, non-church religious associations, women's groups, sports and recreation, as well as local community associations on issues such as poverty, housing, and racial equality, all of which are more relevant to assessing the civic and political engagement of post-1960s generations than the old-fashioned church and political organizations on which Putnam focuses. Indeed, those like Wuthnow who have used more relevant participatory information for the US such as engagement in human rights and environmentalist activities have also revised the Putnam thesis.

One important omission from Putnam's analysis gives a strong indication of the kind of selectivity that underlies his whole exercise. Putnam's focus is on the overall decline in trust; he has little to say about the large differences in civic trust exhibited by privileged and marginalized groups. Research suggests that there is a huge difference in trust between whites and African Americans: the mean percentage of trust among blacks for the whole period is only 17%, compared with 45% for whites. Indeed, one conclusion drawn by other researchers is that much of what Putnam regards as a general decline in trust in the last 20 years of the 20th century in America is explained by declining levels of trust among those whose lives became more difficult and insecure, especially in conditions of growing social inequality.

For the UK, Hall's analysis reveals a large gap in trust between the middle and working classes in relevant British surveys. The better-off exhibit higher levels of trust than the unemployed, those on low incomes, those with insecure jobs and in generally deprived and declining neighbourhoods. And analysis by Letki of data from England and Wales on ethnic diversity found some lack of trust between ethnic groups, but shows that the biggest contribution to negative interaction and attitudes between neighbours is made by the general socio-economic quality of neighbourhoods.

This finding is also very relevant to the debates around David Goodhart's argument that diversity undermines support for the welfare state, and the 'white working class debate', both of which are discussed in the next section.

Putnam's chosen villains, especially dual-career families and television, can also be interpreted quite differently as part of a remaking of modern societies that is not necessarily detrimental to 'community' and 'social capital' as such, but which creates different forms of social networks and a reconfiguration of older patterns of male domination, cultural deference, and youth activities.

Underlying Putnam's anxieties, and those of European governments too, is nostalgia for a somewhat mythical golden age of communal unity, leading to an over-emphasis on common cultural values. Again, this is a significant consideration when interrogating UK government proposals on community cohesion.

Local research on the processes of community formation amongst new migrants in Britain carried out by Roger Zetter and his colleagues shows why a simple contrast between bonding and bridging capital, and the discouragement of the former amongst migrants, is not a satisfactory policy response. In other words, only encouraging 'cohesion' between different communities within the framework of common values and norms of reciprocity and so forth misses the point that many migrant groups still need to organize in a way that allows them to access local welfare resources and employment opportunities. Common national or ethnic origins – Romanian or Kurdish, for example – become the almost inevitable bases for networking and organization, especially where racist hostility is encountered and when there are felt to be distinctive cultural needs and preferences in health care, education, and religion that need to be expressed.

Research carried out in Tottenham in North London and Moss Side in Manchester by Maria Hudson and her colleagues also shows how it is not only important for groups such as Somalis to organize separately, but also why Somali women's groups have been springing up and have actually been helpful in the wider integration of Somali women, with some of the women moving on from more specific concerns to organizing their involvement in the local carnival. Obviously, this is not a form of 'bonding capital' that has dire consequences for social or community cohesion; 'Bosnia' or 'Northern Ireland' are far from the inevitable scenarios that follow from allowing these forms of solidarity.

All in all, the concept of social capital, like the concept of community, appears to be a flimsy foundation for policy-making and cannot provide the basis for moving the agenda beyond forms of multiculturalism, a move which I regard as necessary.

3. The white working class and the problem of 'fairness'

On the 14 October 2009, John Denham, at the time the communities minister in the UK government, announced the start of a £12 million scheme targeted at mainly white working-class areas in various parts of the country. Special community forums were also to be set up to allow local people to air grievances. The grants and the measures were explicitly designed to prevent white working-class feelings of resentment at being unfairly treated in comparison with immigrants from feeding a growing trend for such communities to vote for the Far-Right British National Party. Already, two BNP members, including the leader Nick Griffin, have been elected as Members of the European Parliament, and the party has won a number of seats in local council elections.

In December 2009, Denham berated the middle classes for not understanding the impact of immigration on poorer workers, because they were insulated from competition for jobs and resources. They could therefore feel 'culturally enriched' by migration; but working-class people experienced pressure on jobs, housing, and training opportunities and had an understandable 'sense of unfairness'.

Of course, the reports into the 2001 disorders had all highlighted that the white communities of the Northern cities, especially the working class and poor, had consistently expressed a strong sense of anger at what they thought was the unfair allocation of public funds to projects for the Asian communities compared to the provisions being made for them. All the local authorities had denied this, pointing out that they had been scrupulously fair in the way grants had been allocated.

After 2001, the resentment of the white working class became an issue in a related but distinct debate in Britain. It stemmed from an essay, 'Too Diverse?' by David Goodhart, editor of the influential Centre-Left journal *Prospect*. Goodhart drew mostly upon American arguments that had proposed that immigration and ethnic diversity (and subsequently multiculturalism) in the USA had prevented the development of the kind of collective solidarity that might have led to the creation of a strong European-type welfare state. The similarity in reasoning between the Putnam thesis and this argument is obvious. Goodhart extrapolated from this interpretation of American history to draw the conclusion that immigration and growing diversity (and by implication, the multiculturalism that celebrated diversity) were undermining the kind of common culture, trust, and solidarity that had earlier allowed a culture of sharing to develop and had undergirded the British welfare state.

The basic assumption underlying Goodhart's thesis is that citizens – and he seemed to have the white working class particularly in mind – are likely to be supportive of welfare benefits only to people who seem similar to themselves in values and lifestyle. The more different the culture of their neighbours, and the less the sense of shared history, struggles, and a collective contribution to the welfare state, the less strong the feelings of empathy, sympathy, and solidarity that the indigenous white population would feel towards immigrants and their descendants when it came to state support.

There are serious problems with Goodhart's initial thesis, as pointed out by Banting and Kymlicka, Parekh, Taylor-Gooby, and many other researchers. For one thing, not unlike Putnam, Goodhart posits a mechanical, inevitable trade-off between general social or national solidarity and ethnic diversity. But no such deterministic relationship is discernible historically. Goodhart draws heavily on the American example, but, even if his thesis is valid there, it is not at all clear that it can be transposed on to European nation states. As Taylor-Gooby has shown, the presence of relatively strong Left and labour movements, and the fact that the welfare state had already been established or was set up only as mass non-European immigration was beginning, means that in Europe growing ethnic diversity, which in the USA enabled hostile groups to divide the labour and welfare coalitions before they could establish welfare regimes, has not been able to have the same effect. Support for the welfare state remains high in European countries despite immigration. Parekh and I have also pointed out that in Britain, especially, non-European immigrant labour provided essential support for the creation of the welfare state; it was in the period of Mrs Thatcher's neo-liberal ascendancy that immigration was severely restricted, while the welfare state suffered some of its worst cutbacks. Moreover, welfare states have been under pressure all over Europe, with restructuring and cuts occurring in all of them whether they have had higher or lower rates of immigration.

Goodhart remains more or less silent on multiculturalism, although the implications of his views are clear. However, as Banting and Kymlicka have pointed out, multicultural policies, in so far as they help shore up support for ethnic diversity, can ameliorate the possibly corrosive effects of immigration, again showing that there is no inevitable trade-off between diversity and solidarity. The effects of immigration and ethnic diversity are mediated and can be positively affected by political and policy initiatives that create a more hospitable climate in the receiving population, and are heavily influenced by local conditions of scarcity of resources such as housing, schooling, and employment.

This is where the white working class question re-enters the equation, in the context of a somewhat different playing out of conflicts around immigration, ethnic diversity, and the welfare state. In the UK, this debate, already prefigured in the 2001 Reports, has resurfaced much more strongly with the publication of a widely discussed and controversial study of London's changing East End: *The New East End: Kinship, Race and Conflict* by Geoff Dench, Kate Gavron, and Michael Young, published in 2006.

The study's narrative encapsulates a scenario played out in myriad local areas in Britain and has exercised considerable influence in governmental thinking on community cohesion and new policies towards the white working class, as witnessed by the

announcement of the Communities Minister with which this
section began.

The *New East End* story, in outline, is as follows. Between 1971
and 2001, the population of Tower Hamlets who were of
Bangladeshi origin went from 2% to 30% of the total population of
the borough. The period also witnessed extensive 'white flight'
and displacement, with a growing number of white working-class
East Enders moving to surrounding areas in the county of Essex to
get away from the immigrants and their descendants. Other,
usually younger, white working-class East Enders have had to
leave because of severe shortages of public housing or affordable
private accommodation, to join earlier generations who were
re-housed in Essex in the aftermath of post-Second World War
reconstruction and redevelopment.

By and large, the study paints a picture of acute hostility,
resentment, and sense of betrayal by whites at what they see as
the grossly unfair treatment meted out to them, while newcomers
have had all their needs met. In particular, the authors tell us
that the white working-class population is seething with anger at
the new culture and practice of entitlement according to need
rather than contribution to local and national wealth. The older
generation of whites has also been concerned that their
contribution to the war effort appears to have been forgotten in a
new period of greater concern for immigrants and newcomers.
To their dismay, the white working class saw the welfare state
changing character. The principle of need, especially housing need,
began to trump the virtues of 'waiting your turn' on a ladder on
which length of waiting time was rewarded, as were family ties, so
that sons and daughters of existing residents had priority.

The authors suggest that the collapse of employment in the
docks and other manufacturing in the 1970s and 1980s coincided
with Bangladeshi men deciding to bring over their families,
fearful for them during the war with Pakistan and anxious to be

united with them before restrictive immigration legislation made it more difficult or even impossible. At the same time, the new needs-based system of state welfare allocation was combined with the centralization of power in the hands of middle-class local authority workers, many of whom dismissed working-class complaints as simply racist.

Moreover, the expansion of the financial centre, the City, also located in East London, meant an influx of 'yuppies', for whom the area was merely a playground for cosmopolitan tastes in food and exotic locals, but who had no ties to the local communities and could leave as and when they chose, while their new luxurious housing consumed precious space and fuelled further local anger and resentment amongst the long-standing white working-class residents.

To add insult to injury, as it were, many second- and third-generation British Bangladeshi children, having been given extra help to learn English and settle into English life, had begun to do well in schools, attended universities, joined the professions, and moved out into much better housing in the suburbs.

It is not surprising, the authors argue, that 1993 saw the first election of Far-Right British National Party councillors in local areas, voted into office by sections of the embittered white working class who felt left behind, ignored, and betrayed by new political elites and governing classes.

But the *New East End* study has been severely criticized for providing an over-simplified and misleading account of the events as well as the reactions surrounding changes in the area since the 1970s and 1980s. Here I am drawing particularly upon critiques by those who have worked as local authority officers in Tower Hamlets, as well as various sociologists and geographers, especially Michel Keith, who had been a Labour leader of Tower

Hamlets Council while also being a Professor at Goldsmith's College, University of London.

First, there is a serious omission of important contextual information by Dench, Gavron, and Young. Although their study spanned a decade, the white residents who are quoted are never placed properly in time and place. No indication is given of when, and exactly where, the white residents were making their comments, thus homogenizing them into a mass and failing to give any account of the specific circumstances, such as localized resource shortages, provoking their remarks.

This compounds the error of homogenizing the white working class in another misleading way. The 'whites' are actually a mixture of people of Irish, Polish, Maltese, Greek, and Greek and Turkish Cypriot origin, combined with descendants of the English of rural origin, the remaining descendants of Eastern European Jewish refugees, and newer arrivals from the European Union. There is no singular 'white working-class community' whose views can be treated as unified and articulated in an undifferentiated manner.

Also, there is a tendency to treat the poorest sections of the working class, those most affected by shortages of housing, jobs, and other resources, as synonymous with the whole white working class. This has also been true more generally of popular media coverage of this issue, where the poorest whites are often compared to the ethnic minorities as a whole, ignoring the class divisions within both sets of communities. For example, in comparing educational achievements, the poorest whites are compared to all British Asians or all working-class British Asians.

Minorities are unified in other misleading ways in the *New East End* study. The area also has immigrants and their descendants from the Caribbean and Africa. The local dynamics cannot be encapsulated in an account that simply pits whites against

Bangladeshis. Moreover, there are cross-cutting ties that unite and differentiate the white and minority populations in a complex manner, especially along faith lines: the area has Catholics, Anglicans and other Protestants, Jews, and various types of Muslims.

There is no mention either of the fact that there had been a significant improvement in services and schooling in Tower Hamlets. So much so that the local social services department's strategic partnership scheme had been praised as the 'best in the country', and the national local authority watchdog, the Improvement and Development Agency, had given Tower Hamlets an award for excellence in 'community cohesion'.

Even more damaging is the omission of considerable evidence of discrimination against Bangladeshi immigrants by the local council, especially in housing allocation. Indeed, the complaints against the council's earlier acts of discrimination, including the allocation of the worst housing to Bangladeshis, had reached the point where the Commission for Racial Equality launched a formal investigation, and in September 1987 the CRE served a non-discrimination notice against Tower Hamlets. This seemed to have little effect; in 1991, the High Court issued a non-compliance notice against the council. Similarly, there is mention of racist murders of Bangladeshis, but this does not translate into any serious discussion of the long struggle the Bangladeshis had to mount simply to be able to walk the streets of Tower Hamlets with a modicum of safety.

It is especially surprising that little is made of the fact that so much of the shortage of council housing, the key source of local conflict, had much to do with the selling off of public housing under Mrs Thatcher's 'right to buy' policy, which was introduced in Tower Hamlets in 1980. The policy transformed the previous pattern of housing tenure. In Tower Hamlets in the 1970s, there were something like 40,000 council tenants, with 20,000 other households. By the year 2000, the 'right to buy' had reduced council tenancies to 20,000. In the *New East End* narrative, such growing shortage of public resources is taken for granted without any examination of why there was such acute scarcity.

The *New East End* story has been played out all over the country. As Steve Garner has pointed out, the 'right to buy' policies nationally meant that between 1971 and 2002, the level of home ownership rose from 49% to 69%, but the proportion of households renting council houses fell to 14% from a high of 34% in 1981. Research by Garner and his colleagues in various parts of the country has also picked up a strong sentiment of loss, betrayal, and unfairness felt by white working classes as they compete for scarce state benefits, especially in the arena of housing, but not just in housing.

And we get from Garner a point made consistently by a number of other commentators on the whole debate about the white working class. While the *New East End* and the BNP narratives see the whites as losing out to immigrants, Garner and the others argue that it is to the middle and upper classes that the white and ethnic minority working classes lose out. Interestingly, Kate Gavron, one of the authors of the *New East End* study, has now come round to the same view of shared deprivation relative to the middle classes. But the sense of unfairness felt by the white working class continues, and will do so until the more balanced narratives about their shared deprivation with ethnic minority communities in relation to the middle classes is circulated more strongly and convincingly.

Is community cohesion the problem and the answer?

The concepts and evidence underpinning official policy formation of community cohesion have not survived critical interrogation particularly well.

But in any case, how is community cohesion to be defined, and how is the lack of cohesion to be repaired? Urgency was added to the challenges of 2001 by protests against the invasion of Iraq in 2003, which were partly attributed to British Asian Muslim disaffection and lack of loyalty to the British state, and in particular the July 2005 bombings in London carried out by a small group of radicalized, Islamicist young British Asian Muslim men.

A Community Cohesion Unit was established in the Home Office soon after the 2002 Building Cohesive Communities report; Community Cohesion Pathfinder Programmes have been set up; local authorities have to prepare community cohesion plans which set out how cultural contact between different communities will be fostered and barriers between them dismantled; and relevant research projects have been set up with the involvement of charitable and voluntary organizations such as the Joseph Rowntree Foundation, the Runnymede Trust, and the Heritage and Lottery Fund.

Various governmental agencies have provided several, overlapping definitions of community cohesion, drawing originally from academic papers by Forrest and Kearns. Recent (2006) guidance to local authorities lists the following three features as constituting community cohesion:

1) a common vision and sense of belonging for all communities;
2) those from similar backgrounds have similar life opportunities;
3) strong and positive relationships are being developed between people from different backgrounds and circumstances in the workplace, in schools, and within neighbourhoods.

Many, if not most, commentators and researchers remain sceptical of official thinking on 'community cohesion'. We have already seen that doubts can legitimately be expressed about the degree of separation and segregation between different ethnic groups.

Moreover, the communitarianism underlying governmental proposals, the heavy official reliance on social capital theory, and the legitimacy of the white working-class sense of unfairness have also proved to be very questionable foundations for supporting the agenda of community cohesion.

In addition, there are three key areas of weakness in the community cohesion agenda.

Firstly, and perhaps the most pervasive criticism of governmental policies, is that they only pay lip service to the issue of common class inequalities between ethnic minorities and the white working-class communities that live in close geographical proximity to the ethnic minorities. Although the importance of equal life opportunities is always mentioned in governmental documents, little is said about how inequalities in opportunities are to be overcome, and there have been no serious proposals for overall redistribution of wealth and income.

As all the research shows, especially in response to Putnam's ideas on social capital, the lowest levels of trust between communities and in government are to be found in the poorer areas. While schemes for local regeneration are useful, it is clear that they need to work in tandem with policies for redistribution, given that the period since the 1980s has seen a striking increase in inequality in incomes and wealth and a stalling in rates of upward social mobility.

One index of greater inequality and the privatization of more permeable urban spaces lies in the mushrooming of gated communities, as the wealthy build luxury housing and amenities, protected by intense private security measures. There is more genuine segregation and the living of 'parallel lives' between sections of the wealthy and the rest, especially the working class of all ethnicities, with detrimental consequences for social cohesion and the creation of an even greater sense of exclusion amongst the working classes of all ethnicities.

The absence of serious inroads into socio-economic inequalities means that, in effect, there is what has come to be called a 'culturalization' of policies of community cohesion. The cultures of ethnic minorities and the poor tend to carry the blame for lack of community cohesion. Moreover, governmental discourses slide around between a view of commonality as attachment to neighbourhoods and the poorly articulated 'Britishness' that has also become important in community cohesion debates. Here too, as we shall see, it is the minorities who bear the brunt of rhetorical blandishments to adhere to national values.

While these general criticisms have much force, we need to turn to more detailed research projects that have begun to enquire into issues of community cohesion at local levels. They provide a richer evidential basis for assessing the viability of strategies for moving beyond multiculturalism.

One of the best of these has been carried out by Mary Hickman and her colleagues, researching areas in English, Irish, and Scottish cities. Their research strongly supports the view that both 'relational' and 'structural' issues and initiatives are crucial to the creation of cohesion and solidarity between communities. The view that it is only a matter of addressing structural disadvantage – poor local resources, unemployment, poverty, and so on – as suggested by many of the critics of community cohesion policies, is shown to be misleading. There is no one-to-one correspondence between deprivation and poor community relations.

In some areas, for example, new arrivals and past immigrants were not subjected to racist bullying and harassment; local conditions and cultures have been crucial. For one thing, some areas had a strong local narrative based around the notion that everyone was from 'round here' and culturally homogenous (in contrast to other locales that had developed a conception of the area containing 'people from here and elsewhere'). The localism worked against the creation of friendly neighbourly relations with ethnically distinct newcomers. On the other hand, such insular local cultures showed the capacity to shift their attitudes and behaviour in the wake of sensitive and well-thought-out initiatives by local agencies.

Several such policies stand out. Firstly, where the arrival of newcomers was accompanied by extra resources which benefited all communities, attitudes to immigrants became less hostile and more accommodating. The new resources were deployed in the context of providing better information and 'myth-busting' on the spread of funding between communities. Secondly, local authorities that created recreational and other spaces for intercommunal interaction managed to improve social relations. Thirdly, local agencies that specifically worked with groups such as women to improve access to resources for all communities reduced hostility and created changes towards better relations with new neighbours.

Moreover, forums created to allow freer discussion of difficult interethnic situations allowed a greater diffusion of tensions. In Leicester, this function was performed by the city-wide Multicultural Advisory Group. Crucially, this body has included BBC Radio Leicester and the widely read local newspaper *Leicester Mercury*.

Leicester provides an interesting example of the management of the new 'superdiversity'. The arrival of Somalis, often middle class in origin and who had initially settled in the Netherlands and Denmark, into the highly ethnically diverse area of Highfields had led to considerable hostility between Somali youth and already settled youth of African Caribbean origin. Initiatives in Leicester schools and elsewhere were mobilized. But their success owed much to the fact that the local council had already employed large numbers from ethnic minorities who were able to act as mediators.

This example also underlines an important shift in perspective that is encouraged by the research report. There is not only a 'white backlash', especially against the new immigration. It is long-settled communities from all ethnic backgrounds, including African Caribbeans and Asians, who resent newcomers, whether they are black, as in the case of the Somalis, or white, as with the new European migrants from Poland and elsewhere. Note, too, that the research uncovered racist attitudes from the new Eastern European white immigrants towards blacks and Asians, which was also being addressed in Leicester, especially at the school level.

Interestingly, in the light of many derisory comments from critics of such projects, cultural festivals and other joint cultural activities, such as women cooperating to produce crafts and textiles, were found to have generally beneficial effects. The critique of the 'culturalization' of ethnic relations policies can be taken too far.

There is much else of value in the findings of this research project. I would like to reiterate, though, the conclusion of the researchers that each locale has unique characteristics, something also borne out by research by Les Back in London. Leicester is therefore not necessarily a model in the sense that all its initiatives should be replicated everywhere. Also, there is little doubt that there is much greater continuing racialized hostility in Leicester than is recognized in the research.

It is worth remembering too that intercommunal projects face considerable difficulties in reconciling diverse needs, expectations, and experiences which have become hardened over considerable periods of time. Such projects require patience and long-term perspectives. Those involved in such projects, such as the community worker Alison Gilchrist, have warned against government policies based on targets and rapid results.

Clearly, there is no one simple framework and set of practices that can provide answers to the conundrums of developing 'community cohesion', and the general vagueness of the notion itself leaves much room for variety and local improvisation.

It was encouraging to see that in its final years New Labour thinking was taking on board the sorts of conclusions reached in the local research of Hickman and her colleagues. Thus a more sophisticated official approach can be found in the report *Our Shared Future* (2007) in response to the London bombings of July 2005. The document evinces serious understanding of the importance of local contexts, emphasizing that no single strategy can be prescribed for all neighbourhoods, that there is thus no automatic correlation between deprivation and interethnic hostilities. Areas that experience high levels of conflict usually have multiple issues to deal with, especially the combination of a rapid influx of new workers in an area of low employment opportunities and a shortage of housing. And it welcomes the plurality of identities that individuals now have, creating cross-cutting ties.

Chapter 5
National identity, belonging, and the 'Muslim question'

National identity, belonging, and citizenship

If 'integration' is replacing multiculturalism in Europe, the question has always arisen: integration into exactly what? Or, in terms of the British idea of 'community cohesion', cohesion based on precisely what? Apart from the problems discussed earlier as to how to measure integration and decide when integration has taken place, sceptics have always pointed out that in Britain, say, does integration for immigrants mean aspiring to and succeeding in joining the culture of binge drinking or obesity or xenophobia that are also part of 'being British'? What does becoming British, or Dutch, or any other European actually mean?

The issue, in other words, has become inextricably bound up with the idea of *national identity*. Integration and cohesion have always implied that ethnic minorities and new immigrants need to abide by and take pride in whatever is considered to be the 'core', the defining essence, of the particular nation into which they have been granted the privilege of entry and, eventually, full membership. The nation has become even more centrally the focus because of the centrifugal pressures on its integrity resulting from the forces of globalization, European Union harmonization, and internal nationalisms that had long been contained by the settlements and compromises that had created viable nation states in the first place. And the UK has, for example, been an explicitly multinational state experiencing growing discontent at English hegemony over the Scottish, Welsh, and Irish components.

And then there is the 'Muslim question'. Much of the debate, all over Europe, has been driven by anxiety over the supposed lack of integration and national loyalty on the part of immigrant Muslim minorities, fuelled of course by 9/11 and the rise of radical Islam, the Madrid bombings, the disorders in Britain and France in predominantly Muslim areas, and the involvement of a very small minority of British Muslims in Al-Qaeda-inspired activities, most notably the London bombings of July 2005.

I shall discuss the Muslim issue in the next section of this chapter. For the time being, it is important to disentangle some of the complex and rather bewilderingly confused strands that have emerged in debates over integration and national identity.

The idea of 'core values' has been the most common way of discussing national identity. In Britain, there has been much lamenting that the nation does not have the defining framework of the French '*liberté, égalité, fraternité*' or the American 'land of the free'. So, in major speeches and documents, Tony Blair and Gordon Brown in particular have attempted to lay down templates, in terms of core values, for describing what it is that defines the uniqueness of the British.

In what became a major defining speech on Britishness in December 2006, the then prime minister Blair produced several variations on a theme: 'belief in democracy, the rule of law, tolerance, equal treatment for all, respect for this country and its shared heritage'; 'solidarity, of coming together, of peaceful co-existence'; 'tolerance, solidarity across the racial and religious divide, equality for all and between all'. He insisted too that these values do not dispense with multiculturalism completely. There is a right to 'our own different faiths, races and creeds'; but we have a 'duty to express any difference in a way fully consistent with the shared values that bind us together'.

Trawling through Gordon Brown's various statements yields a view composed of three main elements. Firstly, 'the days of Britain having to apologize for our history are over ... we should celebrate much of our past ... our history [is] at the core of our Britishness', and one conclusion to be drawn from Britain's entanglements with the world is that Britain is 'outward-looking' and characterized by 'openness and internationalism'. Secondly, an emphasis on liberty, fairness, and tolerance as defining British values; and thirdly, considering 'duty' as an abiding value.

Brown also mentioned 'adaptability', 'hard-headed commonsense', and a 'deep suspicion of fundamentalism'. These last characteristics obviously chime even with Left and Centre-Left historians such as Hobsbawm and Colls, but Colls also points to the significance of military victories and a contradictory combination of 'English liberty at home and British power abroad'.

And here we have one of the first and major difficulties involved in defining an over-arching Britishness that focuses only on the positives of a long, complex, and contradictory history. No nation on earth has only positives in its past, however much its members may want to believe otherwise. The historian Linda Colley was much nearer the mark when she pointed out that the 'English, Welsh, Scots and Irish have all ... been greedy, pushy, intrusive traders and warmongers, aggressive, violent, frequently oppressive, often arrogant and perfidious'. She doesn't mention racism and often brutal colonialism. As Marquand puts it, 'There is an ugly side to Britishness as well ... A conversation on Britishness that ignored the dark side of empire would be a travesty.'

And combined with the fact that, as many others have pointed out, 'dissent' and 'radicalism' have also been enduring features and have contributed much to present-day liberties, equality, and tolerance, the Blair and Brown versions cannot provide any kind of singular, coherent narrative that every citizen can 'sign up to' as the current phrase has it. Indeed, there is obviously no such narrative in any nation's history. In Britain, it is hard to see monarchists and republicans, liberals, socialists, and conservatives, the religious-minded and humanists, feminists and believers in 'family values' – to identify only some of the standpoints along the ideological fault-lines of British culture – agreeing to a common narrative except at a level that would be bland, ridden with platitudes, and vulnerable to disintegration in the face of serious discussion of any specific period or set of events.

Indeed, it is actually more productive to admit to a lack of consensus and to accept that this is not just a strength but positively a requirement for a healthy democracy, as many political theorists such as Tully, Mouffe, and Amin have argued.

But there are other serious questions confronting the Britishness project as currently framed. What exactly is 'British' about any of these values? The Dutch (who pride themselves on their tolerance as a national virtue) and other nations that have attempted to provide a list to which ethnic minorities and new immigrants might sign up have come up with very similar items. This is hardly surprising. Any liberal democratic polity or nation state will expect, at the least, a commitment to democracy and to some degree of tolerance, fairness, and equality amongst its citizens (although serious disagreements arise everywhere whenever any attempt is made to put substance into what are relatively empty ideas and ideals).

In any case, can senses of belonging and loyalty to the nation, and patriotism, be instilled by citizenship tests and ceremonies, another set of innovations favoured by countries such as Britain and the Netherlands? Especially when many new citizens may already have experienced hostility, rejection, and discrimination, or will soon encounter these? Most historians and social scientists have been sceptical that belonging and genuine affection for a country can be instilled by top-down national measures involving national flags, oaths, and anthems. There is nothing objectionable in principle about such tests and ceremonies – Canada and the USA have had them for a long time, and it is arguable that newcomers learn some useful information about the societies they have migrated to, and that a symbolic marking of entry into citizenship indicates that it is an important transition that deserves celebration, reinforcing some sense that there are rights and responsibilities involved.

However, the necessary engagement of the emotions for the creation of genuine attachments can only come about organically through fulfilling, enjoyable, and memorable experiences and ongoing social interactions which continue to build and reinforce affection and a sense of belonging. All the available evidence suggests that stronger 'consensus' and less diversity, as recommended by social capital theorists, is not necessarily required for what one might call a good-enough sense of belonging and social solidarity amongst members of a nation state.

A more appropriate strategy, one that is also part of governmental projects in the UK and elsewhere, is to 'de-nationalize' and 'de-ethnicize' these issues by framing them within public discourses of citizenship, rights, and responsibilities, which recognize that a variety of identities are compatible with civic commitment and recognition of broad values of democracy, fairness, equality, rule of law, and so forth. And this is not just to accommodate ethnic minorities and new immigrants. For one thing, in the UK, for example, all the evidence suggests that most Scots have minimal attachment to ideas of Britishness and have a particular antipathy to the English hegemony that has characterized traditional conceptions and global projections of

Britishness. Moreover, as many now recognize, a less nationalistic project of civic belonging is far more appropriate to a rapidly globalizing world and one in which the hungry economies of all advanced industrial nation states are going to require, and will experience, continuing migrations in an age of declining birth rates and skill shortages.

In 2002, the UK government introduced citizenship education into the National Curriculum for all pupils aged between 11 and 16, with recommendations also for the inclusion of topics around racism and ethnicity, a variety of faiths, and the study of black and Asian writers in English Literature. But two different sets of criticisms of the new citizenship curriculum have brought into sharp focus the inherent difficulty of constructing one coherent narrative for British history and core values. While a government-commissioned review by Sir Keith Ajebgo complained in 2007 that there was not enough emphasis on UK identity and history, in January 2009, Sir David Watson, Professor of Higher Education Management at the London University Institute of Education, condemned current citizenship classes as 'brittle' and 'nationalistic', calling for more 'international sensibilities'. He also recommended a less culturally specific version of the test for new applicants for citizenship. In particular, the inculcation of patriotism enshrined in the school citizenship was regarded in a study by the Institute as too morally prescriptive, glossing over the 'moral ambiguities' that are part of any nation's history.

Clearly, the project of a de-nationalized process of citizenship is far from having been achieved; it remains an ideal. But in my view, it is one worth striving for. Note, too, that the evidence for a serious decline in national identity is lacking; it is not clear that what needs reinforcing is national belonging rather than a sense of citizenship and forms of empowerment that can foster civic responsibility. Research conducted by Heath, Martin, Elgenius, and others at Oxford University, based on surveys from the 1960s to the present, suggest that the majority of the population continues to have a sense of British identity. But Heath and his colleagues found little relationship between the continuing sense of Britishness and an inclination towards civic duty over the last 45 years or so. Thus, there appears to be a complex relationship between national belonging, social solidarity, and active citizenship.

What has changed is that more members of the population now have at least dual identifications – Scottish and British, Welsh and British, for example. And all the research on settled ethnic minorities also reveals comfortable multiple and transnational belongings, with varying degrees of attachment to 'being British'. This was confirmed in my extensive survey of evidence of changing ethnic minority identities in Britain.

Heath et al. argue that if there is an issue to be addressed here, it is to do with the young black people of Caribbean and African origin, at least one-fifth of whom have a weak sense of British belonging. Research suggests it may have to do with a complex intertwining between class and blackness. Claire Alexander in her seminal study *The Art of Being Black* (1996) has revealed, on the one hand, strong local attachments to cities such as Birmingham and London, and to locales within them, for instance Hackney. Now even postcodes have become part of belonging and territorialization, sometimes to a dangerous degree. However, Alexander's work and that of others also shows that there is a tension between being middle class and being recognized as black. Middle-class accents and aspirations, including working hard at school, are associated by an indeterminate proportion of working-class blacks as a selling-out to 'whiteness' and 'acting white'.

Clearly, this has a destabilizing effect on coupling blackness and Britishness. But something like 20% of those described as 'Caribbean' in surveys have a white partner, 40% of 'Caribbean' children have a white parent, and the category of 'mixed race' is probably the fastest-growing 'ethnic minority' in Britain. All of which confirms the view I have been advocating that identities of all Britishers, but especially those of its ethnic minorities, are complex, unstable, and shifting.

The identities of Britain's Asian minorities are even more complex. Post-colonial divisions of nation and geographical origin have been superimposed on dense, interwoven patterns of identities based on religion, caste, sub-caste, and various other kinds of descent groups, and rural/urban and regional differences, which have made generalizations about Asians an extremely hazardous exercise. Roger Ballard, in introducing a collection of essays on South Asians in Britain points out that what every chapter in the volume illustrates is not only how much each community differs from the next, but also that each is following its distinctive dynamic: 'The result is . . . ever-growing diversity . . . to talk of an Asian community or even "Indian", "Pakistani" or "Bangladeshi" one is often to reinforce a fiction.'

However, it is clear that the main focus of official alarm is directed at Muslim communities, considerably heightened after the July 2005 London bombings. And it is Muslims all over Europe who have been regarded as the most in need of a greater sense of national and European belonging. It is Muslims, above all, who have become the target for programmes of community cohesion and integration in Britain and the rest of Europe. As with national integration and community cohesion in general, have we witnessed a gross over-reaction?

The 'Muslim question'

At the end of 2009, the Swiss voted in a referendum to ban the construction of any more Muslim minarets, in a country that has four such constructions and a Muslim population of 400,000. President Sarkozy of France was a high-profile supporter of the Swiss decision which, however, is widely regarded as being in breach of the European Convention on Human Rights, singling out Islam, as it does, for discrimination. In early 2010, the French denied citizenship to a man of Moroccan origin who apparently forced his wife to wear the full veil. Legislation has been introduced to ban the full veil in public (about 1,000 to 2,000 women are reportedly wearing this form of full covering in a population of 6 million Muslims in France).

To many critics, these decisions confirm that Europe is in the grip of an 'Islamophobia' that is as pernicious as the anti-Semitism that engulfed Europe during the 1930s. Others, taking their cue from Samuel Huntington's deeply flawed but influential book of the same name, regard this as only the latest skirmish in a 'Clash of Civilizations' which has now replaced the Cold War and battles between nation states in a new global battleground. Supporters of the decisions may indeed see this as a hopeful sign that Europe is continuing to fight back against its imminent decline in the face of Muslim immigration, Muslim birth rates in Europe, and global *jihad*, predicted in a whole spate of publications, for example Walter Laqueur's *The Last Days of Europe* (2007) and Christopher Caldwell's *Reflections on the Revolution in Europe: Immigration, Islam and the West* (2009).

The key events in the story of the rise of a more militant and globally conscious Islam since the Islamic revolution in Iran in 1979 and the campaign to ban Salman Rushdie's *Satanic Verses*, itself given great impetus by the notorious *fatwa* against Rushdie by Iran's then leader, Ayatollah Khomeini, are hopefully too well known to require detailed narration here. Nor can I hope to provide anything approaching a comprehensive discussion of the issues that arise in considering the trajectories of Islam in Europe. But there are some general points worth making before embarking on a brief analysis of the relationship of Muslims in Europe to multiculturalism.

First, general discussions of Islam and the 'Muslim question' in a global context, as, for example, in the work of Samuel Huntington, are often unproductive because of what Olivier Roy calls a 'culturalist' conflation and confusion between Islam the religion and Muslim cultures (and, I would add, Muslim identities). As a religion, Islam consists of the Qur'an, the *hadith* (stories about Muhammad's behaviour and sayings not contained in the Qur'an), and the commentaries on both by Islamic scholars. These should not be conflated with, or assumed to determine, the content of Muslim cultures – or 'civilizations' – for 'culture' includes social traditions, urban and rural social structures and relationships, literature, cuisine, political institutions, and so forth. As another noted scholar, Sami Zubaida, has pointed out, it is highly misleading to refer to a 'Muslim society' when what actually exist are heterogeneous Muslim societies in which varieties of Islam the religion play different roles and co-exist with a range of cultural traditions and forms of secularization. Muslims exist in a variety of nationalities and ethnicities, speak in a wide range of languages, and engage in a wide variety of cultural practices. Muslim societies contain huge variability of Muslim identities, from highly religious and politically conservative, to nominally religious, politically liberal, and culturally reformist, and all manner of combinations of these. And this is before we consider the great Sunni–Shia divide and its manifold sectarianisms.

The trajectories and problems of Muslim societies are influenced by much more than just 'Islam'. It is revealing that more secular regimes such as in Egypt and Tunisia have often been as involved in blocking democratic reform as more formally Islamic nation states such as Iran or Saudi Arabia.

These distinctions become even more important in understanding the huge variety of Muslim cultures and identities as they are evolving amongst Muslims in Europe, as we shall see.

A second cautionary point to remember is that, contrary to popular perceptions, 'political Islam' may well be on the retreat. That is, Islamic political movements that emerged in the aftermath of the Iranian revolution of 1979, and which seemed like they were going to sweep all before them, have in fact had to be content with a relatively minor role in domestic politics in the Middle East and elsewhere. The movements have become normalized as political parties – the FIS in Algeria is a good example – and have found themselves campaigning under the banners of democratization, human rights, and the revitalization of 'civic society', all concepts borrowed from Western political discourse. Few command more than 20% of the vote in national elections.

Moreover, even in Iran, the ascendancy of Islamic political forces has not in fact resulted in a reversion to polygamy or the extended family with large numbers of children; and literacy rates amongst Iranian women have risen dramatically since the 1979 revolution, from under 30% to 80%. The majority of university students in Iran are women. In a Muslim nation such as Indonesia, the fertility index in 2000 was only 2.6, lower than in the Catholic Philippines where it was 3.6.

The framing of a global conflict between 'the West' and 'Islam' thus mistakenly homogenizes both. Western countries are also struggling with fundamental issues such as abortion, the role of women and the family, the meaning of patriotism, and liberal versus conservative interpretations of religion, especially as manifested in the debates about the ordination of women and gay priests. The Western obsession with finding and funding a moderate Islam over-estimates the influence of the religion in shaping the societies and misunderstands the divisions within a supposedly united Islamic fundamentalism.

What about global Muslim support for Al Qaeda and other violent Islamic *jihadist* movements? Although fears about Islam and

Muslims are rife in the West, Fareed Zakaria, editor of the respected American journal *Newsweek*, has proclaimed (February 2010) that Bin Laden 'has lost the clash of civilizations'. Only 'a handful of fanatics scattered across the globe' really support Bin Laden-style *jihadism*. Generally, he claims, across the Muslim world extremists have been isolated, no major country looks like it is going to fall to *jihadist* forces, and 'modern, somewhat secular forces are clearly in control and widely supported across the Muslim world'. Zakaria's narrative recounts how condemnations of *jihad* and *fatwas* against suicide bombings have multiplied, from the Al-Azhar University of Cairo, to prominent supporters and mentors of Bin Laden, and the Darul Uloom Deoband movement in India, which had originally given staunch support and inspiration to Al Qaeda.

Zakaria's conclusions are supported by many reliable surveys of Muslim opinion. One of the latest is *Who Speaks for Islam?*, a major compendium of Muslim views from all over the world from Gallup polling over the period 2001–2007, and compiled from several thousand hour-long interviews with individuals in 35 Muslim countries and those with significant Muslim populations.

The surveys reveal much greater admiration for the USA and the West than the 'they hate our way of life' mantra might have us believe. There is considerable desire for greater democratization, a challenge to corruption, and equality for women (even in Saudi Arabia), and a powerful longing for economic development (all of which have been borne out by recent pro-democracy rebellions in Egypt, Tunisia, Libya, Syria, Bahrain and Yemen). On the basis of this extensive survey, only 7% of the population of global Muslims could be regarded as 'radicalized' or 'extremist', based on their view that the 9/11 attacks were 'morally justified'. But even this minority would not necessarily take part in any violence, although it viewed the USA with great hostility. And it is worth underlining that the reasons they gave for supporting the attacks were primarily political rather than theological. And the vast majority of global Muslims regard extremism and a lack of openness to the ideas of others as the traits they most deplore in their own societies.

On the vexed question of *sharia*, or Islamic law, it is notable that while there is considerable support for some inclusion of *sharia* in legislation, the elements of *sharia* that are valued and regarded as suitable are very varied, and belie the stereotype of the bloodthirsty stoning of adulterers and chopping off of the hands of thieves, for which there is little enthusiasm.

The shattering of the myth of a clash of civilizations and stereotypes of global Muslims which emerge from *Who Speaks for Islam?* is also reflected in all serious studies of European Muslims and surveys of Muslim opinion in the West.

It is worth remembering, when considering the question of Muslims in Europe, that they constitute 4% of the population of the European Union, which puts the fears of a Muslim takeover of Europe into a proper context. And, of course, what applies to global Muslims applies to European Muslims: they are not a homogeneous group, but comprise populations that often have little in common, with different national and ethnic origins – for example, mainly South Asian in Britain, North African in France, and Turkish in Germany – and different degrees of religious commitment, attitudes to Western culture, and sense of national commonality with their non-Muslim fellow citizens (and they speak a wide variety of first languages).

It is not surprising that in a recent Policy Exchange Report, 71% of British Muslims aged 55 and over felt that they had more in common with non-Muslims in Britain than with Muslims abroad. And surveys have consistently reported high degrees of feelings of Britishness as a component of Muslim identities. A Channel 4 NOP survey from spring 2006 recorded 82% of British Muslims – who make up 2.7% of the British population – as feeling 'very

strongly' (45%) or 'fairly strongly' (37%) that they belonged to
Britain.

The Policy Exchange Report appears to show considerable
differences between the generations amongst British Muslims,
with fewer of the 16 to 24 age group feeling British (as above), more
of them (37% compared to 19% of over 55s) wanting to send
their children to Islamic schools, with similar differences in
proportions showing support for *sharia* law. Inevitably, given its
conservative standpoint, the Policy Exchange blames
'multiculturalism' for these generational differences, concluding
that multicultural policies have encouraged feelings of
separateness amongst young Muslims.

But there are contrary indications from other surveys. The Open
Society Institute conducted a study of Muslims in 11 West
European cities and published its findings in December 2009. One
of its most interesting findings, very relevant to criticisms of
multiculturalist policies of the type contained in the Policy
Exchange Report, is that 78% of Muslims in the UK cities
identified themselves as British, but only 49% of Muslims
considered themselves French, and only 23% felt German. British
multicultural policies appear to have made Muslims actually feel
more accepted and have fostered a greater sense of national
identification. And in contrast to the Policy Exchange findings, the
Open Society Institute found that levels of what the report calls
'patriotism' are stronger amongst second-generation Muslims.

Low feelings of attachment to French and German national
identities, as compared with British identity, amongst Muslims
stemmed from a stronger sense that they are not accepted by
their fellow citizens and the state, with Germans granting
citizenship rights only in the 1990s and the French banning the
headscarf and generally perceiving a clash between 'Islamic' and
'French' values.

However, focusing on the UK, it is important to try and understand what national identity, Britishness, and citizenship mean to second- and third-generation British Muslims, and whether there are significant differences in this regard between them and their white counterparts. There is some evidence that young white British people, compared to their Muslim counterparts, see their identities more in terms of national culture than citizenship, although whiteness is also a strong taken-for-granted element of their identity. As Bagguley and Hussein have concluded from their study of Bradford and the 2001 disorders, for young South Asians, including those of Pakistani and Islamic origin, their Britishness is couched more strongly in a civic sense of citizenship, with notions of equal rights with all other Britishers as a dominant strand running through their sense of national belonging and identity.

Their feelings of cultural identity are clearly a mixture of parental cultures and British culture. It is common for these to be expressed as complex constructions which combine being Asian, Pakistani, Indian, Muslim, and British in a variable, changing, and contextual manner which belies easy classification. Terms like 'British Asian' or 'British Muslim' simply fail to capture the huge variability in how the second and third generations are fashioning what have been called 'hybrid', 'new ethnicities', except in the crudest possible way.

Islamic youth radicalism

A very common explanation for the Islamization of youth identities is couched in terms of an 'identity vacuum'. This is regarded as a form of social pathology. In the 1980s and 1990s, it was commonly referred to as stemming from the predicament of being 'caught between two cultures', pitting a pre-modern parental one – heavily marked by rural origins in countries like Pakistan, and emphasizing arranged or forced marriages, religiosity, and so forth – against the modern, individualist, 'Western' culture that allowed freedoms and pluralities of lifestyle, especially embedded in youth subcultures. In this highly essentialist earlier 'culture clash' formulation, the hapless second generation was seen as suffering a sort of psycho-cultural breakdown.

The current version of this type of interpretation also posits a culture clash, but now claims that there is not so much a pathological breakdown as an 'identity vacuum' that is being filled, for many in the new generations, by a radical, fundamentalist, and puritanical Islam, reflected in women's adoption of the headscarf and men's excessive religiosity and desire for life under *sharia* law and the establishment of a global Islam.

But there is no 'identity vacuum', at least not in the sense implied in this sort of interpretation. What the newer generations have done, again, is to forge myriad new identities, with a bewildering mixture of religions, class and youth cultures, musical tastes, and fashion statements. The young British Muslim women I referred to earlier, wearing *hijabs* and also immersed in rock music that expresses their complicated rebellion, represent only one of a wide range of complex, fluid, unpredictable combinations of identities that have been created out of the cultural resources that young Muslims find themselves growing up with in European cities.

One of the differences, though, is a greater disengagement from conventional political processes, although in this they are little different from their white fellow young citizens. A good introduction to the variable and complex identities of young Muslims in Britain – including the turn to the world of drugs – can be found in a number of studies, including those by Philip Lewis, M. Y. Alam, and Anshuman Mondal. Lewis's discussion of the Muslim Youth Helpline and City Circle are particularly interesting in giving accounts of free, open debates amongst young British Muslims about a wide range of topics, with many contributions by educated and professional young Muslim women.

Clearly, though, for some young Muslims, a militant Islam is the response to their dilemmas, and for a very small number, this Islamism has been the springboard into armed conflict, whether that has taken the form of suicide bombings in European cities or travelling to fight in Afghanistan, especially, but also Iraq, Chechnya, and other front lines where Islam is regarded as being under occupation and attack.

The numbers involved are small. In the UK, the current official estimate is of about 2,000 individuals, or less than 1% of British Muslims, who are regarded as at risk of serious involvement in violent actions. The appeal of militant Islam is somewhat wider than this, although difficult to quantify. A joint report commissioned by the British Foreign and Commonwealth Office concluded in 2004 that two types of young Muslims were particularly open to sympathy for, and sometimes actual recruitment by, militant Islamist groups:

> By and large most young extremists fall into one of two groups: well educated undergraduates or with degrees and technical professional qualifications in engineering or IT; or underachievers with few or no qualifications, and often a criminal background.

The report also notes that many come from liberal, relatively non-religious Muslim homes where the parents are bewildered by the radical path taken by their children, and that it is not unusual for commitment to radical Islam to develop only in adulthood. Small numbers are white British converts (and, of course, there have been several cases of white Americans) and those of African Caribbean origin who have grown up in the West Indies. Some have been converted and radicalized in prison. This is akin to one common trajectory amongst other young Islamists: finding in Islam an identity and way of life that provides a route out of disillusionment with what is regarded as a particular 'Western' trap of drugs, alcohol, and crime. This is particularly reflected in the biography of the ringleader of the 7/7 bombers, Mohamed Siddique Khan.

Currently, there are two very different ways of understanding this phenomenon, in addition to the model of identity vacuum and psycho-cultural breakdown that I have already criticized. On the one hand, many popular media and political interpretations label those involved as mindless fanatics and fundamentalists, determined to destroy 'our' (Western) way of life, and who are beyond comprehension except as manifestations of 'evil', influenced by state-sponsored ideologies and organizations orchestrated by states constituting an 'axis of evil' in Bush's notorious phrase. The only appropriate response is to wage a 'war on terror' against them.

A quite different framework, derived from the work of historians and sociologists such as Olivier Roy, Max Farrar, Alana Lentin, Michel Wieviorka, Sarah Glynn, Gabriele Marranci, Sami Zubaida, views the phenomenon of Islamic radicalization amongst young Muslims in the West in particular as an understandable *political*, rather than merely religious, response, and certainly not as a pathology. Questions of pathology may have some relevance when the biographies of those who actually commit acts of suicide bombing are considered. But note that the 2004 report's advice to the FCO and the Home Office consistently emphasizes the fact that neither religion *per se* nor individual pathology are the really significant drivers: the report stresses instead that British Muslims suffer three times the level of unemployment as other British citizens, that they live in the most deprived areas of the country, and experience not only disadvantage but also discrimination. And the report mentions several times that there is anger amongst young Muslims about Western foreign policy, especially in relation to Palestine–Israel, Afghanistan, and Iraq.

Interpreting Islamism amongst British and European youth as a form of political radicalization means that this phenomenon can be seen, in part at least, as akin to the Left-wing radicalization of the young during and after the 1960s in Western Europe and North America.

However, the difference this time is that the radical and revolutionary Left has little of the appeal and influence that kept drawing in young radicals in the earlier period. Left ideologies have been replaced by the appeal of a deterritorialized and global 'pure Islam' untainted by the cultural syncretism and political compromises of national versions of Islam in countries like Pakistan, Morocco, and Egypt. Young Muslims have also become detached from established mosques, and from older leaders and foreign imams with little understanding of dilemmas confronting young British Muslims.

The rise of the Internet has, of course, been crucial to this attempt at creating a new Muslim *ummah*, or global community, with ideological texts, sermons, and recruiting videos now easily available. The creation of global networks and 'communities' enables the development of forms of organization and activism unimaginable in an earlier era.

The predominantly Muslim youth involved in the disorders of 2001 in Britain, and others more drawn to radical Islam, should also be seen in a different context, as forming part of a series of events and spontaneous movements involving inner-city youth from a variety of ethnic minority groups. In the 1980s, it was youth of African Caribbean origin who fought pitched battles with the police and protested vigorously against discrimination and disadvantage. In the 1990s and the first decade of this century, it is Muslim youth. Again, this is a way of seeing young Muslim radicalization as a mainly political phenomenon, but with some religious underpinnings.

Elements of masculinity also come into play. Involvement with Islamist movements gives a religio-revolutionary twist to the 'tough', street-wise image of rebellion, even incorporating, according to researchers such as Macey, more local cultural references such as 'tough Northern/Yorkshire lad' into the mix that forms the collage of the radical Islamist persona.

The ideologies of Islamism also provide anti-imperalist and anti-capitalist elements reminiscent of earlier Marxist critiques, further reinforcing the persuasiveness of the comparison with the general youth radicalization of the 1960s. Anti-imperialism is fed by denunciations of Western involvements and interventions in shaping events in the Middle East, most recently the invasions of Afghanistan and Iraq, and by the continuing anger at the West's double standards in not bringing Israel to account for violations of UN resolutions or condemning their nuclear arms. The anti-capitalism intertwines with the critique of consumerism that is explicit in the puritanical religiosity and the revulsion against the commodified sexualization of popular culture in general, and women in particular, that is central to the new Islamicism. As Lewis recounts, for example, the radical group *Hizb ut- Tahrir* was able to lead a local Muslim campaign to ban the opening of a pornography bookshop in Stoke on Trent. Anti-imperialism and anti-capitalism also come together in critiques of Western companies using sweatshops in Muslim countries such as Bangladesh to mass-produce cheap fashion garments for Western markets.

However, as emphasized earlier, there is no simple, direct line of connection between socio-economic disadvantage and Islamic radicalization. As researchers and government agencies are only too well aware, it is not only working-class Muslim youth who have become involved in radical Islam. There appear to be just as many middle-class, university-educated young Muslims, more often than not with a scientific, medical, or engineering background, who have become attracted to radical Islam in the West (and in the Arab world and now even Nigeria).

Note, too, that radical Islamist groups like *Hizb ut-Tahrir* have attractions for some Muslim women as well. They have perhaps strategically taken a more liberal stance on Muslim women's desires for not entering into arranged marriages, for going on to higher education, and of course involvement in politics, thus providing an avenue of protest and alternative Islamist justifications for pursuing non-traditional lifestyles.

Anxiety persists within sections of European populations and for their political representatives, as well as for intellectuals, journalists, and others, that Islam and liberal democracy are impossible partners and that integration into Western polities and national democratic institutions requires wholesale transformations in the beliefs, lifestyles, and political orientations of Muslims in particular, rather more than for those of other ethnic minorities and minority religious groups. And of course, multiculturalism has been held responsible for allowing and encouraging Muslims to supposedly keep themselves separate and alienated from mainstream institutions and liberal beliefs.

How much credence should be given to such misgivings about Muslims in Europe?

European Muslims, secularism, and democracy

Radical Islam, as we have seen, appeals to a very small minority of European Muslims and Muslims globally. But is there nevertheless a special problem of Muslim integration in Europe? One reason why many have replied in the affirmative is because Muslims appear not to subscribe to the distinction between the public and private realms that is central to the modern Western idea of secularism; Muslims appear to be demanding special cultural recognition and special group rights from what is otherwise a culturally neutral state and public sphere. On closer inspection, though, the scale of this and related problems appears to have been exaggerated. For example, it has been argued that Muslims are demanding special treatment when they have requested *halal* meat in school canteens or have wanted to wear the headscarf at work. These demands, it is said, breach the long-accepted division between a culturally neutral, universalist public sphere and a more culturally particularistic private sphere. But of course, as the women's and gay movements have successfully argued in parallel, the public sphere only appears to be neutral, and is in fact thoroughly permeated and structured by male, heterosexual norms.

The Western notion of 'the individual' as the basis of public life in liberal democratic societies has historically smuggled in the male as the model of what the individual's characteristics. For example, this individual never appears to be burdened by the special circumstances of pregnancy, breastfeeding, or childcare, and heterosexuality has been the norm, such that the acceptance of same-sex partners in public life has required a massive cultural shift in the acceptance of homosexual relationships. Similarly, this individual has always been modelled on the norm of a Christian (more often than not Protestant) person in relation to public holidays of religious origin or dietary regulation in schools, or facilities and time for prayer at work. Also, when Muslims have demanded the right to official recognition as a national religion in European states, they have been asking for no more than equality with the Jewish, Catholic, and Protestant religions. This has now been acknowledged in Europe, and official status has been granted to Islam in France, Germany, the Netherlands, and elsewhere in Europe.

Similarly, the demand for Muslim faith schools has not been a request for special treatment, but equality with the freedoms enjoyed by Jews, Catholics, Anglicans, and others. Evidence suggests that most of the Muslim faith schools that have been established in France and Britain have been meeting stringent National Curriculum regulations and have managed to attain good academic standards. Interestingly, too, John Bowen, who conducted research in faith schools in France, provides many illustrations of the inculcation of good civic norms of tolerance and neighbourliness and law-abiding behaviour in Muslim schools, which makes such institutions positive vehicles for Muslim integration rather than the alienation and separation of Muslims from the mainstream. However, research on all faith schools in the UK by the Runnymede Trust found that there was too little engagement with responsibilities towards a community cohesion agenda, and little serious dialogue with other faiths. This was not a special 'Muslim problem', but one embedded in schools from all the faiths. As the abolition of faith schools is not on the agenda, even in France, all such schools need greater regulation to ensure a wider religious curriculum and instil a genuine commitment to liberal democratic citizenship norms.

Attempts by Christian groups to ban films such as Mel Gibson's *The Passion of Christ* (2000) highlight that the tension between fundamentalist religious groups and liberal practices of freedom of artistic expression is not confined to Muslims. However, it is quite obvious that at least some sections of European Muslim populations seem to find critical representations of Muslims or Islam in the arts unacceptable, and this is likely to create flashpoints and illiberal backlashes – even murderous violence, as in the case of the Dutch film-maker Theo van Gogh. On the other hand, it is also clear from the Danish cartoons affair that some sections of the European intelligentsia are determined to engage in gratuitous provocation in order to create a public fear of a specific Muslim threat to free expression. In the case of the Danish cartoons depicting Muhammad, for example, it is worth pointing out that the editor of *Jyllands-Posten*, the newspaper that originally published the demeaning portrayals in 2006, had in 2003 refused to publish cartoons about Jesus on the grounds that they would offend Christians. And a French court in October 2005 had ordered the removal of posters that depicted the Last Supper in what was thought to be an offensive manner. Unfair double standards do seem to exist in many quarters where there is a willingness to protect Christian sensitivities but not those of Muslims.

There is a broader issue here. The modern European nation states reflect a variety of compromises around religion and, subsequently, national and ethnic minorities, that evolved after the Treaty of Westphalia of 1648 that ended the catastrophic wars of religion in Europe. The growing Muslim presence in Europe has coincided with a gradual unravelling of some of those compromises and, in the sphere of religion in particular, has opened up fissures that were regarded as long buried under an irreversible tide of secularism. It is clear that Western nation states are in a transitional stage when new accommodations are required, and indeed are gradually being developed.

It is worth noting that lively debates are under way amongst European Muslims about how Islamic injunctions are to be interpreted in the new context of more secular and liberal national cultures. Issues of democracy, gender equality, the public–private distinction, interest-bearing loans (forbidden under strict Islam), greater individualization of religious practice, and so forth, are now being creatively re-thought and accommodated to conform to Islamic norms while meeting the needs of new generations seeking greater clarity on how to be 'good Muslims' while living lives also shaped by commitment to gender equality and other liberal values.

Even in France, a survey in 2006 found that 74% of all French people think that there is no incompatibility between being a devout Muslim and living in a modern society, and French Muslims are as likely to emphasize their national identity over their religious one as are US Christians, and more likely than most other European Muslims.

Conclusion: Moving on: multiculturalism, interculturalism, and transnationalism in a new global era

Has multiculturalism failed?

It seems obvious that European nation states have decided that the period of multiculturalism is over. Multiculturalism seems now to be regarded by governments, intellectuals, and large sections of the national populations as either disastrous or at least a serious wrong turn in the response to immigration by non-white populations, usually from former colonies of the European powers in the period after 1945 at the end of the Second World War.

But is this really the whole story? In this book, I have presented reasons to doubt whether the account presented above is as persuasive as it might first seem. The view that the whole era of multiculturalism has been a serious wrong turning is difficult to sustain when examined against the available evidence that I have presented. Even the flaws that have been revealed do not necessarily lead to the conclusion that multiculturalism has been a disaster or even a major mistake. To some extent, because of the coincidence between the more permanent settlement of the newer, 'post-war' ethnic minorities and what in the Introduction I have called the 'triple transition' – the loosening of the bonds within the

Western European nation states, the emergence of post-industrialism, and the restructuring of the welfare state – these immigrants and the multicultural policies that developed in response to them have too often been blamed for the overall national cultural fragmentation and changes to national identity, and the inner urban unemployment, housing shortages, the pressure on education, health, and other public services, that have in fact been more the result of the huge transformation wrought by the triple transition, itself intertwined with newer, more accelerated forms of globalization and the growing importance of transnational structures such as the European Union.

The level of minority alienation from national culture and identity is much higher in countries such as Germany which operated a 'guest-worker' system and where there has been great official resistance to incorporating cultural diversity into the narrative of the nation. France, as we have seen, has managed to instil Republican citizenship values into the minorities, but the absence of serious official recognition of ethnic minorities, including the half-hearted nature of equal opportunity policies, has bred acute resentment in the name of citizenship rights, while the official resistance to identity symbols such as the headscarf has been driving sections of the large Muslim minority into a more hard-line retreat into Islamic identities. Apparently paradoxically, this retreat has been particularly marked amongst young Muslim women.

Increasing levels of inequality and growing class differentials have been more important than multicultural policies in creating social distance and breeding resentment within and between various ethnic groups, although the area-based bidding process for funding urban projects in the UK, and attempts by local authorities to channel funding into especially faith-based community projects, has combined with housing shortages and misleading local media reporting to entrench divisions and fuel resentment.

Post-1945 immigrants in all the Western European states came to work in industries like manufacturing and textiles which have suffered serious decline. Levels of unemployment and poverty have risen dramatically in these areas. The brunt of the economic collapse has actually been borne by ethnic minorities in so far as their levels of unemployment and poverty have risen faster and higher. In the *banlieues* of France and the northern towns of England, Muslim youth especially have typically twice or three times the levels of unemployment as youth from the majorities. And their communities have been sinking into poverty at an alarming rate.

It has often been argued that a key problem with multiculturalism has been its inability to make significant inroads into the socio-economic disadvantage and discrimination suffered by ethnic minorities, reflected in their poor educational achievements and high levels of unemployment. But the main cause of high unemployment amongst ethnic minorities, especially the youth, has been the collapse of the older industries in the urban centres to which their parents and grandparents had originally migrated. A relatively detailed picture of the devastation of de-industrialization in Britain's northern cities, and particularly its impact on ethnic minority youth, was painted by the 2001 reports which I have discussed at some length in Chapter 3. Remember too that the reports – together with numerous other studies – identified racial discrimination in the public and private sectors as important contributory factors to the employment and housing situation of the minorities.

All the Western European countries are characterized by high levels of ethnic minority youth unemployment and overall levels of poverty. But there are variations, and they do not correlate with the adoption of multicultural policies. The UK, Germany, and Austria have a better record on minority unemployment than the Netherlands and Sweden, as the political scientist Randall Hansen, amongst others, has pointed out. The UK, the

Netherlands, and Sweden have all adopted multiculturalism, as we have seen, to a greater degree. And the lack of multiculturalism in France, in the form of robust equal opportunity policies, according to most informed researchers, has contributed to the high levels of minority youth unemployment, and there is official hostility to the recognition of ethnic minorities and the collection of statistics on their fate. More effective anti-discrimination and equal opportunity measures in both public and private sectors, in the UK in particular, appear to have contributed to a better record on ethnic minority unemployment than elsewhere in Europe. In the UK, students from Indian and Chinese backgrounds have overtaken their white counterparts in school achievement and university attendance, but this has much to do with their higher social class origins and histories before migration.

The arrival of asylum-seekers and refugees and newer migrants from Eastern Europe and the emergence of what has been called 'superdiversity' appear to have put a particular strain on housing, schools, and the health service in some areas, allowing the Far Right an opportunity to intensify anti-immigrant sentiments. In Britain, there is a growing recognition that the benefits and strains of immigration are unevenly spread, with some working-class areas and communities bearing the brunt of increased competition for scarce jobs and public resources, while the benefits are often reaped only by employers and middle-class families who have been able to refurbish their properties more cheaply and obtain cleaners and other domestic workers. Multiculturalism has little to do with any of these processes, although in some cases the lack of preparedness on the part of local authorities and central government has been papered over by attempts of some official agencies to simply laud the resulting 'cultural diversity' without tackling the resource strains imposed by rapid inward flows of new migrants. But this is a *post hoc* multiculturalism which has not actually been the cause of the problems. One fundamental requirement is the provision of more resources, although this is unlikely in the new period of austerity, presenting grounds for pessimism.

If multiculturalism cannot be said to have failed – indeed, in some cases it has not even been wholeheartedly attempted – is there any need to move on? I think that there is a need to now take a somewhat different path, a point with which I will conclude.

There is, though, the question of liberalism and its relation to multiculturalism. In particular, there is the unresolved issue of free speech and freedom of artistic expression and to which there is no definitive resolution. A major misgiving, even on the part of those who have supported multiculturalism, stems from their belief that some or other version of cultural relativism, and the consequent practice of complete respect for all cultures, has led to a stifling of open debate in the name of 'political correctness'.

The Salman Rushdie affair, the killing of the Dutch film-maker Theo van Gogh, the furore over the Danish cartoons of Muhammad and the withdrawal of a play by a Sikh author depicting events in a Sikh place of worship, the Gurdwara, have been some of the best-known flashpoints for this debate. Arguably, Rushdie and his supporters were too arrogant in their initial response to Muslim concerns, Theo van Gogh's film and the Danish cartoons were gratuitously provocative, and the operation of double standards whereby Christian sensibilities have had greater protection against offence can all be pointed to as mitigating circumstances.

Nevertheless, there is, in my view and those of many others sympathetic to some of the core principles of multiculturalism, a genuine issue of many ethnic minorities being unable to freely tolerate criticism and open discussion of matters of faith, and this will obviously have to change if these faith communities are to be at greater ease with more secular, liberal cultural contexts. And arguably, the minority communities have had too few internal debates about these issues; the matter requires and deserves serious attention and wide discussion in the range of forums now available within these communities. This is one reason why, and one of the areas in which, multiculturalism needs to move on.

However, the inroads made by demands for the teaching of creationism and 'intelligent design' in the school curriculum in Britain and the USA show that knotty issues around secularism, liberty, and the place of faith and religious belief involve more than just Muslims, other ethnic minorities, and multiculturalism. Faith schools continue and show every evidence of thriving; it is to be hoped that there is tight regulation to ensure that they foster genuine interfaith dialogue and a positive approach to the benefits of a liberal, pluralist, secularist accommodation between the religious and other spheres.

Is multiculturalism in terminal retreat or actually dead?

In the USA, despite decades of 'culture wars', the general principle of multiculturalism appears now to be firmly embedded, especially in education and the national narrative. As Glazer, a distinguished conservative student of ethnic relations, explains the meaning of the title of his book *We Are All Multiculturalists Now*:

> I mean that we all now accept a greater degree of attention to minorities and women and their role in American history and social studies and literature classes in schools. Those few who want to return American education to a period in which the various subcultures were ignored, and in which America was presented as the peak and end-product of civilization cannot now expect to make any progress in the schools.

And in the UK and elsewhere in Western Europe, it is worth remembering that not all public media debate has been dominated by those who wish to bury multiculturalism. Support has been forthcoming from what would appear to be unlikely sources. Britain's premier Centre-Right publication, *The Economist*, is one such, decisively rejecting in 2007 what it calls the tendency for 'multiculturalism' to become as derogatory a word as 'neo-con' or 'socialist'. Deriding the habit of aiming at easy targets such as forced marriages and honour killings, the article penned under the regular by-line of Bagehot argued that the limited segregation that was taking place between ethnic minorities could largely be blamed on the arenas of housing and education policies that may have carried some of the attributes of multiculturalism, but in circumstances where enforced mixing would have been counterproductive. Bagehot argues, too, that the success of growing sections of the ethnic minority populations and the level of Britain's integration of ethnic minorities compared to levels in other Western European countries also suggests that the adoption of multiculturalist policies in the UK has been a boon rather than a liability. Small groups of disaffected Muslim youth, it argues, have emerged out of intergenerational conflict and high levels of unemployment and deprivation in de-industrialized areas; multiculturalism has little to do with these trends. And relatively high rates of black–white marriage also suggest less cultural separateness than in other countries, especially the USA.

Similar arguments have also been put by Anthony Giddens, one of the key intellectuals behind New Labour's 'Third Way' project, who has also, unlike New Labour's politicians, come out in support of multiculturalism in 2006. He argues, amongst other things, that much of the debate about multiculturalism has been 'crass, ignorant and misconceived', pointing to the failures of the Far Right in the UK compared to other European countries such as Denmark, Belgium, France, and the Netherlands as evidence that Britain has been the most successful EU state in managing cultural diversity. Echoing the 2001 reports, although he does not refer to them, Giddens calls for 'more multiculturalism, not less'. Here, he echoes the sentiments of many informed commentators in the Netherlands and France, as I have pointed out.

Moreover, liberal governments, despite all the official distancing from the era of multiculturalism, have remained more committed to it than might seem to be the case, citizenship tests notwithstanding.

Vertovec and Wessendorf have rightly pointed out that much of this distancing is rhetorical, with support for 'diversity' now replacing the language of multiculturalism. And a great deal of the original multicultural framework, and most of the policies, remain firmly in place. There has been no withdrawal of commitment from equal opportunity policies nor any attempt to water down any existing anti-discrimination legislation. Cultural recognition remains a contested issue, with the headscarf ban in France and the resistance to mosque-building in Switzerland being notable examples, but arguably no more so than before and still confined to countries where multiculturalism has always been weak. Despite the fears of many, there has been no straightforward or wholesale stampede into assimilationism; an ethos of cultural pluralism and diversity is still being publicly promoted, albeit within the somewhat tighter constraints of forms of integrationism. But the integration measures are relatively mild. As Randall Hansen remarks, requiring citizens to learn the national language cannot be regarded as a threat to multiculturalism, and the same might be said for learning basic facts about national culture (quibbles about the relevance of particular facts and issues aside).

The essays in Vertovec and Wessendorf's collection reveal that cities across Europe, including Copenhagen, Stuttgart, Vienna, Zurich, and Dublin, have embedded diversity principles into their policies and practices. Multiculturalism survives, but with the clear notion that practices such as female genital mutilation or forced marriage are simply not permissible, something that was clear too from the recommendations of the Report of the Multi-Ethnic Commission in Britain in 2000 (better known as the Parekh Report).

It would be a mistake to believe that 'backlash discourse' against multiculturalism does not have effects, especially on interethnic relations. Moreover, the election of a Conservative–Liberal Democrat coalition in the UK is showing some danger signs for the future of multiculturalism in so far as Conservative members of the government have shown a desire to reshape the school curriculum in a more nationalist direction, with a positive gloss on Britain's imperial past, and to withdraw the Human Rights Act based on the European Convention on Human Rights and replace it with a diluted British bill of rights. It is unlikely too that all of the community cohesion initiatives and funding from the previous Labour government will survive, especially in the face of a programme of drastic cuts in public expenditure.

However, despite even stricter controls against non-EU migrants, it is very likely that a general British commitment to 'diversity', although a bland notion open to different interpretations, will be maintained. The more established forms of interethnic and interfaith consultation and general support for equal opportunities for ethnic minorities will likely continue, although there will be even less mention of multiculturalism in official discourse. At the time of writing, it is not clear what the coalition's support for 'The Big Society' means for interethnic relations.

Towards interculturalism

It is clear, all caveats notwithstanding, that a policy and ideological shift has taken place throughout Europe. But this is not always a move away from multiculturalism; sometimes it is a transformation beyond multiculturalism into forms of what might be called 'interculturalism', a term that has already made its appearance in official discourses and has been particularly popular in Germany.

One statement that signals the difference of emphasis involved in interculturalism, beyond multiculturalism, is to be found in the European Union's seventh principle in the list of 'Common Basic Principles for Immigrant Integration' (2004): 'Frequent interaction between immigrants and Member State citizens is a fundamental mechanism for integration', and the statement goes on to mention 'Shared forums, intercultural dialogue, education about immigrants and immigrant cultures', and so forth.

The key point here is that instead of a mere celebration of diversity and different cultures as in versions of classic multiculturalism, what is involved here is the positive encouragement of encounters between different ethnic and faith groups and the setting up of dialogues and joint activities. This has also, of course, been the thinking behind policies of community cohesion in the UK. At one point, the British government had even suggested to local councils that they should not fund single-community projects, concentrating their resources instead only on projects that brought communities together, but this proposal was dropped as imposing too rigid a requirement. In its place came a recognition that such funding decisions should be made at local levels, especially because single-community organizations also played a vital role in integrating communities into mainstream culture and intercommunal participation.

Of course, this should not be taken to imply that intercultural dialogue was not part of previous multicultural philosophy and practice. But there is now a definite recognition that the idea of multiculturalism has succumbed too easily to an interpretation of ethnic cultures as having strictly definable boundaries, having unchanging essential components, and lacking quite fundamental internal dissent. Multiculturalism, in other words, has been too prone to essentialism, although it does not necessarily entail it.

The 'multi' in multiculturalism immediately gives too much leeway to the space that has always existed in 'multiculturalism' to enable a slippage into thinking of ethnic and national cultures as having rigid boundaries. Use of the notion of interculturalism acts, instead, to undercut this essentialist tendency – it cannot by itself completely prevent it – by building in a conception of connectedness, interaction, and interweaving between the beliefs, practices, and lifestyles of different (not separate) ethnic groups as part of national cultures that are in constant flux because of myriad changes produced by a wide range of technological, economic, political, and cultural factors (the Internet and accelerated globalization having been two of the most significant in the last decade). In this respect, my proposals share some elements with Hollinger's suggestions for how the USA should move beyond multiculturalism by adopting a 'post-ethnic' perspective.

'Interculturalism' also avoids a tendency that multiculturalism has inadvertently encouraged, the treatment of all non-Western cultures as sharing little with Western cultures and ideals, and wholly separate from the West in their development. By contrast, at the heart of any form of interculturalism is a clear recognition of the historical, and even more the contemporary, connectedness of cultures on a global scale, as well as the shared values that have developed independently in different geo-cultural spaces in the history of the planet.

Even in multiculturalist narratives, the profound historical interconnectedness between the West and the non-West has often been submerged, instead giving rise eventually to the absurdities of Huntington's conception of a world order that has been the outcome of, and is still defined by, a so-called 'clash of civilizations'.

This rigid distinction between the 'West and the Rest' relies on a misleading history that posits the West as having unique features which supposedly developed independently of other, non-Western cultures and are said to have been a central part of the West's contribution to civilization, and indeed part of its 'civilizing mission', both during and after the period of European imperial expansion and colonization of large parts of the globe. This narrative of the rise (and justified global domination) of the West, now led by the USA, asserts that democracy, tolerance, freedom, the rule of law, egalitarianism, conceptions of human rights, individualism, scientific rationality, humanism, even towns, universities, and the idea of romantic love, are all uniquely Western. They have emerged, so the argument goes, from a unique concatenation of ancient Greece and Rome (classical Antiquity), Christianity (especially the Protestant Reformation), the European Renaissance and Enlightenment, the scientific and industrial revolutions, and modern Western democratic movements. The 'East', including Islam, on the other hand, is seen as intrinsically authoritarian, based especially on Confucianism in the Far East and rigid Hindu notions of caste in the Indian subcontinent, and Islamic opposition to secularism, humanism, and scientific inquiry.

The historical basis for this hubris has been thoroughly discredited by less Eurocentric accounts. For present purposes, I will make a few points drawn from the work of Jack Goody, the distinguished Cambridge anthropologist and comparative historian, and the Nobel Prize-winning economist and philosopher Amartya Sen, although by now a large number of other serious scholars have also contributed to this 'decentring of the West', as it is sometimes called.

Let us take, first, the issue of humanistic scepticism towards religion and divinity. In India, atheistic schools of thought flourished in the 6th century BC, at the same time as agnostic Buddhism emerged and began its long march through China and other parts of the Far East and South-East Asia. Other key Indian texts such as the *Ramayana* and the *Upanishads* contain views sceptical of religion, the divine, and life after death, and their influence continued in Indian traditions of thinking.

Nor is tolerance a uniquely Western notion. The Indian emperor Ashoka articulated a well-thought-out idea of tolerance as early as the 3rd century BC. There have also been prominent Islamic advocates and practitioners of tolerance. The 16th-century Moghul emperor Akbar accepted and encouraged human rights such as freedom of worship and was against forced conversions. The Muslim Ottoman Empire is a particularly well-known example of religious tolerance, its *millet* system allowing religious communities to exist under their own legal jurisdiction. And Christians, Jews, and Muslims flourished side by side in the famous 'golden era' of Islamic Spain in the medieval period.

What is now taken to be the Western idea of freedom is a post-Enlightenment development. Aristotelian ideas of freedom for an upper class – excluding slaves, women, and some others – are to be found in a range of Asian conceptions, including those supportive of the caste system which involved protection for Brahmins, and in China, where there was protection for the freedom of Mandarins. And in traditional African societies, even if there is no equivalent of the word 'freedom', there is obvious awareness of the status of those who are slaves and subordinates and those who have greater autonomy. The authoritarianism of Chinese and other cultures has been much exaggerated, partly by misunderstanding the complexity of different strands within Confucianism, and also by ignoring the influence of the more egalitarian Buddhist cultural components.

And amongst many other violations of the human historical record, describing the rule of law and property rights as Western inventions is only possible if their existence in oral and other agricultural societies is simply written out of global history, as innumerable anthropologists and historians have pointed out.

The Greeks may have invented the word 'democracy', but certainly not its practice. Goody points out that 'the desire for some form of representation, to have one's voice heard, is intrinsic to the human situation' and refers to a range of cultures in Africa and elsewhere that relished their freedom from chieftainship and central state control. He remarks that historically even the most authoritarian governments have had to take account of popular sentiments and demands. Mesopotamia had city states very like those of ancient Greece. And in Europe, democracy did not acquire definite positive valuation until the 19th century.

The idea of the West as the unique fount of all that is politically progressive can only be believed if modern versions of Western institutions are read back illegitimately into extraordinarily oversimplified and selective interpretations of classical Antiquity and other periods of European history, and by ignoring similarities between Western and non-Western societies in relation to democratic and other progressive developments.

Wholesale divisions between the West and the Rest also rely on ignoring the essential connectedness between cultures and the extent to which developments in the West borrowed from non-Western cultures.

At the very least, it is now clear that Indian, Arab, Chinese and Persian mathematicians, philosophers, logicians, astronomers, medical researchers, and others made discoveries that were fundamental to the subsequent flowering of Western science, and that while Europe had sunk into what have been described as the Dark Ages, Chinese and Indian sciences and manufactures were flourishing, and agriculture as well as urban design and living were far in advance of anything in the West. No wonder that even in 18th-century Europe, in the period of the Enlightenment, Chinese, Turkish, and Indian cultures and lifestyles were much admired and often more favourably regarded than their Western counterparts. We now know, too, that the European

Renaissance which preceded the Enlightenment owed much to scholars who had worked in Islamic societies and had preserved, translated, and built upon the philosophical and scientific achievements of the Greeks. And classical Antiquity was not born without interconnections and borrowings from other cultures and regions, especially those of ancient Egypt. Whatever the detailed criticisms that might be levelled at Martin Bernal's widely discussed *Black Athena*, where the debt to Egypt is particularly emphasized, there can be little doubt that it is mistaken to see the flowering of classical Greece as simply generated from within, and certainly not as a separate 'European' phenomenon.

'Rationality', often taken to be the preserve of the West, has been a collective, global human achievement in which the West has for long periods lagged behind the Rest, a point forcefully made in Goody's aptly titled *The East in the West*.

Goody argues convincingly, drawing upon a wealth of research from other historians, that instead of making rigid distinctions between the authoritarian East and the decentralized, individualistic West which led to the so-called 'European miracle' of industrial civilization, it makes more historical sense to talk of 'the Eurasian miracle', of societies sharing a Bronze Age legacy, but in which a not completely unique West gained advantage partly by way of superior military and naval technology. The West, borrowing much from the Rest in technology, science, and culture, came to dominate parts of the globe that had for centuries been more economically and technologically advanced, sharing many social features such as marriage systems and ethics which had allowed trade and manufactures to flourish in the East. That period is now coming to an end, as some Eastern economies now seem poised to take over, and shift the pattern of dominance and supremacy further over to the East, as had been the case earlier.

Western imperial expansion and colonization in the 18th, 19th, and early 20th centuries had a profound impact on countries such as India and in the Arab Middle East, creating extraordinary hybrid cultures where Western languages, literatures, forms of governance, and institutions such as modern universities combined to create societies which were able to fight in Western wars, eventually fought themselves out of direct colonial rule, and were then able to provide the cheap labour which made a vital contribution to the post-Second World War prosperity of the Western European economies.

The populations that came from the previous colonies had already been deeply marked by these previous interchanges with the West, despite governmental and popular concerns that these were 'dark strangers' devoid of civilization. 'They' were 'coloured' 'ethnics' who supposedly arrived into cultures with wholly different but universalist liberal and democratic values and institutions.

This formation of Western identity, creating a sense of its uniquely civilized character, in opposition to the wholly different non-West, has now been thoroughly deconstructed, especially in the field of 'post-colonial studies'. However, note a particular insight from this flourishing field of research. It has emphasized how the formation of the European nation states was deeply affected by their colonial and imperial projects. What Foucault famously called 'governmentality', the government of populations in a systematic form – with the use of specially collected information, relevant experts, and ever more detailed surveillance, including the use of fingerprinting, which the British pioneered in India – had its origins in methods developed to govern the colonies. The need for systematic mass and elite education to provide disciplined labour as well as cadres of civil servants also has colonial connections. In Britain, even the use of English literature as a form of education and 'civilization' was tried first in India, and only then imported back as an educational technology into Britain.

In other words, it was not the case that European nations were formed first without reference to the colonies and only then had their institutions imposed on colonial societies; the very form that European nation states took was massively influenced by institutions that were first developed to govern the colonies.

There is now an urgent need for a transformation of the vocabulary of multiculturalism into that of 'interculturalism', with a corresponding shift to underpinning premises which highlight the deep historical interconnectedness of cultures and an understanding of how conceptions of tolerance, liberty, rationality, and so forth are shared across 'civilizations', and in particular how non-Western cultures have made a vital contribution to the development of these ideas and their appropriate institutions. Modernity is not a uniquely Western phenomenon, but a shared Eurasian achievement.

Seeing non-Western immigrants as no more than pre-modern diluters of a uniquely Western way of life is a major obstacle to developing a more appropriate ethos and institutions for managing the 'superdiversity' of European nation states in the 21st century. The centrality of dialogue to a new ethos of interculturalism requires not just a bland respect for 'other cultures', but an understanding of how much is shared already and how these commonalities provide a basis for developing more common understandings.

None of this is to underplay the degree to which there continue to be differences in the way liberties, rights, sexuality, and civic behaviour and responsibilities are conceived and practised amongst different communities of culturally diverse European nation states. But once it is accepted that histories are interconnected and shared, that supposedly unique Western forms are actually joint non-Western and Western achievements, that all ethnic communities including the ethnic majority are themselves divided over the appropriate interpretation of rights, liberties, sexualities and civic conduct (think of conservative reservations about abortion, homosexuality, women priests and so forth across the different ethnic groups and faiths) and that newer generations of non-Western immigrants are rapidly developing new hybrid versions of the cultures of their parents and those of 'Christian Europe', the idea of separate, whole, 'Other' cultures and 'Our' cultures begins to look more and more inappropriate.

We are now part of an era of ever-expanding 'transnationalism' in which the interconnections between migrants, their descendants, and their previous 'home' countries are becoming more complex, and in many cases are intensifying because of the rapid development of cheaper telephony, airline flights, and the Internet. National and ethnic minority identities have been changing in response to more intense globalization, and the proliferation of multiple identities has now been widely documented. This is allied to a new 'cosmopolitanism' in which many members of minorities and majority populations are becoming more adept at code-switching between cultures, lifestyles, and languages. Such processes are inevitably uneven and dependent upon such factors as class and levels of income, gender, and age. Nevertheless, it is becomingly increasingly obvious that previous nation-state-centred perspectives are in need of replacement by ones that are more attuned to denser patterns of global interconnectedness.

In this new transnational, cosmopolitan phase, a genuinely dialogic interculturalism within state borders is not only more vital but also more possible. Parekh's version of dialogic multicultural philosophy, set out in his *Rethinking Multiculturalism* provides an initial platform, one that he has developed more appropriately, incorporating more recognition of interconnected histories, new disaporas and their hybrid and multiple identities, and new cosmopolitanisms within nation-state populations, in his recent *A New Politics of Identity* (2008).

What is to be the fate of concepts like integration and community cohesion? 'Integration' has always been undermined by the inability to specify adequately what integration is supposed to be into, except in the broadest sense of Western values such as liberty, tolerance, and so forth that are in fact the site of debates and uncertainties, especially in relation to concrete policies and civic behaviour. And both integration and 'community cohesion' appear to posit unrealistic end states of stasis and consensus which, as Tully, Amin, and others have pointed out, are inimical to pluralistic, democratic cultures with healthy, vibrant debates. Although there must of course be relatively stable rules of debate, engagement, and resolution of controversial issues, both the rules and the solutions always have to be left open to reasoned and reasonable challenge. The goal would be to create accommodations between ethnic groups and other communities that also create a sense of 'we-ness' rather than serve to entrench sentiments of 'us' and 'them'.

In conditions of scarce resources and established cultural hostilities, funding for leisure, sports, and other communal facilities, housing, the sites for the building of mosques, temples, and synagogues, will be subject to conflicts that can only be constructively dealt with if relations of trust, mediation, and compromise are built up over time in suitable forums of discussion. I have cited several initiatives in cities such as Leicester and elsewhere that provide routes forward in this regard.

The fact that there can be broad agreement on the need to subscribe to general values such as tolerance, cultural diversity, individual rights, and so forth, a consequence of actually existing interconnectedness and interculturalism, makes the task of finding acceptable compromises a little easier. Complete incommensurability between cultural groups in values and meanings is rare and even less likely with new generations growing up in multiethnic settings. However, interculturalism does not require that all citizens subscribe to the same narrative of the nation's history – indeed, all nations are divided over their own histories – and solutions to most practical issues that arise in multiethnic contexts do not need this sort of tight consensus.

Lessons can be learned from regions as wide apart as Northern Ireland and Gujarat where, as research by Hewstone and Varshney respectively shows, civic associations have been built up to create mixing and enough sense of common belonging to prevent or repair fractures between neighbourhoods and ethnic and faith communities. Ethnographic research from a range of urban centres including Vancouver also show how bottom-up negotiations and friendships amongst neighbours allow the creation of forms of multiethnic amiability that Hibbert has called 'Cosmopolitanism at the local level', although this is not a linear process but one which over time also changes in character with succeeding generations.

Interculturalism should be seen as an *emergent process* with no necessary end point. The project needs an acute awareness that interethnic mixing and dialogue may also lead to more conflict in the short term, and that formal interethnic contact is more productive in carefully planned and constantly monitored and managed contexts. Lessons are available from a large number of case studies, but each situation is unique and requires local knowledge and local initiatives and democratically decided forms of interethnic activities and discussions. On the other hand, at both local and national levels, there will obviously have to be a more tolerant approach to the multiplicity of identities that characterize populations in a more transnational age. In particular, there is no compelling reason why national loyalty, for example in sports, should always trump other loyalties

And there are generalizable processes and institutional forms such as the 'transformative accommodation' championed by Ayelet Shachar and continual 'dialogue between diversity regimes' advocated by Grillo. The latter cites the manner in which Hindu

5. Dialogue between people, as in the *Mixen aan de Maas* project in Rotterdam, can be effective in breaking down barriers

and Sikh demands for crematoriums to accommodate some of their funeral rites in Britain have been dealt with by the courts and local authorities as a good example, and perhaps model, of how interethnic dialogue can lead to compromises acceptable to all sides. The best source of examples of recent intercultural projects in Europe and North America is Phil Wood and Charles Landry's *The Intercultural City* (2008). The initiatives discussed range from Burnley Youth Theatre to Oldham Unity in the Community sports programme, Danish libraries, Vancouver's community houses, Rotterdam's *Mixen aan de Maas* project, and Turin's 'creative management of conflict' project which puts 'intercultural mediators' on the street to work with young people, street traders, new arrivals, and established residents 'to understand emerging trends, anticipate disputes, find common ground and build joint enterprises'. Turin's first cohort of eight workers originated from Algeria, Congo, Morocco, Serbia, Peru, Brazil, and Italy: just the kind of group required to deal with the emerging 'superdiversity' that characterizes the new cities of Europe and North America too.

Interculturalism, though, requires adequate funding, just as did multiculturalism. And it cannot by itself address issues of racism, ethnic minority inequalities, nor wider class and gender inequalities which are vital to multiethnic civility and the preservation of social bonds in increasingly privatized, consumerist societies facing the challenges of de-industrialization, separatist regional demands by substate national minorities, and drastic cuts to welfare services. Interculturalism also requires that bridges are built along cross-cutting lines of gender, age, and a variety of other identities and interests; it must move away from a world which privileges ethnicity and faith above all other forms of identification. And it leaves untouched the global inequalities which are major drivers of the migration of people from South to North and East to West.

References

Introduction

B. Barry, *Culture and Equality: An Egalitarian Critique of Multiculturalism* (Polity Press, 2001)

W. Kymlicka, *Multicultural Citizenship: A Liberal Theory of Minority Rights* (Oxford University Press, 1995)

B. Parekh, *Rethinking Multiculturalism: Liberalism and Cultural Diversity*, 2nd edn. (Palgrave Macmillan, 2005)

A. Rattansi, 'Changing the Subject? Racism, Culture and Education', in J. Donald and A. Rattansi (eds.), *'Race', Culture and Difference* (Sage, 1992)

P.-A. Taguieff, *The Force of Prejudice* (1987) (University of Minnesota Press, 2001)

C. Taylor, 'The Politics of Recognition', in A. Gutmann (ed.), *Multiculturalism and the Politics of Recognition* (Princeton University Press, 1994)

S. Vertovec, 'Super-Diversity and its Implications', *Ethnic and Racial Studies*, 30(6) (2007): 1024–54

Chapter 1

Y. Alibhai-Brown, *After Multiculturalism* (Foreign Policy Centre, 2000)

K. Banting, R. Johnston, W. Kymlicka, and S. Soroka, 'Do Multiculturalism Policies Erode the Welfare State?', in K. Banting and W. Kymlicka (eds.), *Multiculturalism and the Welfare State:*

Recognition and Redistribution in Contemporary Democracies (Oxford University Press, 2006)

H. Entzinger, 'The Rise and Fall of Multiculturalism: The Case of the Netherlands', in C. Joppke and E. Morawska (eds.), *Toward Assimilation and Citizenship: Immigrants in Liberal Nation-States* (Palgrave Macmillan, 2003)

A. Favell, *Philosophies of Integration: Immigration and the Idea of Citizenship in France and Britain*, 2nd edn. (Palgrave Macmillan, 2001)

J. S. Fetzer and J. C. Soper, *Muslims and the State in Britain, France and Germany* (Cambridge University Press, 2005)

N. Fraser, 'From Redistribution to Recognition? Dilemmas of Justice in a "Postsocialist" Age', in N. Fraser, *Justice Interruptus: Critical Reflections on the 'Postsocialist' Condition* (Routledge, 1997)

T. Gitlin, *The Twilight of Common Dreams: Why America is Wracked by Culture Wars* (Metropolitan Books, 1995)

R. Hasan, *Multiculturalism: Some Inconvenient Truths* (Politico's, 2010)

W. Kymlicka, *Multicultural Odysseys* (Oxford University Press, 2007)

K. Malik, *From Fatwa to Jihad: The Salman Rushdie Affair and its Legacy* (Atlantic Books, 2009)

B. Parekh, 'Redistribution or Recognition? A Misguided Debate', in S. May, T. Modood, and J. Squires (eds.), *Ethnicity, Nationalism and Minority Rights* (Cambridge University Press, 2004)

B. Prins and S. Saharso, 'In the Spotlight: A Blessing and a Curse for Immigrant Women in the Netherlands', *Ethnicities*, 8(3) (2008): 365–84

M. Schain, 'Minorities and Immigrant Incorporation in France', in C. Joppke and S. Lukes (eds.), *Multicultural Questions* (Oxford University Press, 1999)

K. Schönwälder, 'Germany: Integration Policy and Pluralism in a Self-conscious Country of Immigration', in S. Vertovec and S. Wessendorf (eds.), *The Multiculturalism Backlash: European Discourses, Policies and Practices* (Routledge, 2010)

C. Taylor, 'The Politics of Recognition', in A. Gutmann (ed.), *Multiculturalism and the Politics of Recognition* (Princeton University Press, 1994)

S. Vertovec and S. Wessendorf (eds.), *The Multiculturalism Backlash: European Discourses, Policies and Practices* (Routledge, 2010)

Chapter 2

R. Aly, 'My Life as an Undercover Muse-lim', *The Guardian*, 15 February 2010

J. R. Bowen, *Why the French Don't Like Headscarves: Islam, the State and Public Space* (Princeton University Press, 2007)

M. Dustin and A. Phillips, 'Whose Agenda Is It? Abuses of Women and Abuses of "Culture" in Britain', *Ethnicities*, 8(3) (2008): 405–24

A. Hargreaves, *Multi-Ethnic France: Immigration, Politics, Culture and Society*, 2nd edn. (Routledge, 2007)

R. Hasan, *Multiculturalism: Some Inconvenient Truths* (Politico's, 2010)

S. Okin, 'Is Multiculturalism Bad for Women?', in J. Cohen, M. Howard, and M. Nussbaum (eds.), *Is Multiculturalism Bad for Women?* (Princeton University Press, 1999)

B. Parekh, *Rethinking Multiculturalism*, 2nd edn. (Palgrave Macmillan, 2005)

A. Phillips, *Multiculturalism without Culture* (Princeton University Press, 2007)

O. Roy, *Globalised Islam: The Search for a New Ummah* (2002) (Columbia University Press, 2004)

R. Schweder, '"What about Female Genital Mutilation?" And "Why Understanding Culture Matters in the First Place"', in R. Schweder, M. Minow, and H. R. Markus (eds.), *Engaging Cultural Differences: The Multicultural Challenge in Liberal Democracies* (Russell Sage Foundation, 2002)

J. W. Scott, *The Politics of the Veil* (Princeton University Press, 2007)

B. Siim and H. Skjeie, 'Tracks, Intersections and Dead Ends: Multicultural Challenges to State Feminism in Denmark and Norway', *Ethnicities*, 8(3) (2008): 322–44

I. Traynor, 'Feminist, Socialist, Devout Muslim: Woman Who Has Thrown Denmark into Turmoil', *The Guardian*, 16 May 2007

Chapter 3

P. Bagguley and Y. Hussain, *Riotous Citizens: Ethnic Conflict in Multicultural Britain* (Ashgate, 2008)

T. Cantle, *Community Cohesion: A Report of the Independent Review Team* (The Home Office, 2001)

A. Carling, 'The Curious Case of the Mis-claimed Myth Claims: Ethnic Segregation, Polarisation and the Future of Bradford', *Urban Studies*, 45(3) (2008): 553–89

T. Clarke, *Report of the Burnley Task Force* (Burnley Task Force, 2002)

J. Denham, *Building Cohesive Communities: A Report of the Ministerial Group on Public Order and Community Cohesion* (The Home Office, 2002)

D. Duprez, 'Urban Rioting as an Indicator of Crisis in the Integration Model for Ethnic Minority Youth in France', *Journal of Ethnic and Migration Studies*, 35(5) (2009): 753–70

E. Engelen, 'Through a Looking Glass, Darkly', *Ethnicities*, 8(1) (2008): 128–33

H. Entzinger, 'Changing the Rules While the Game is On: From Multiculturalism to Assimilation in the Netherlands', in Y. Bodemann and G. Yurdakul (eds.), *Migration, Citizenship, Ethnos* (Palgrave Macmillan, 2006)

H. Entzinger, 'Different Systems, Similar Problems: The French Urban Riots from a Dutch Perspective', *Journal of Ethnic and Migration Studies*, 35(5) (2009): 815–34

M. Farrar, *The Struggle for 'Community' in a British Multi-Ethnic Inner City Area* (Edwin Mellen, 2002)

N. Finney and L. Simpson, *Sleepwalking into Segregation?: Challenging Myths about Race and Migration* (Policy Press, 2009)

A. Hargreaves, *Multi-Ethnic France: Immigration, Politics, Culture and Society*, 2nd edn. (Routledge, 2007)

A. Korteweg, 'The Murder of Theo van Gogh: Gender, Religion and the Struggle over Immigrant Integration in the Netherlands', in Y. Bodemann and G. Yurdakul (eds.), *Migration, Citizenship, Ethnos* (Palgrave Macmillan, 2006)

M. Macey, 'Gender, Class and Religious Influences on Changing Patterns of Pakistani Muslim Male Violence in Bradford', *Ethnic and Racial Studies*, 22(5) (1999): 845–66

K. Malik, *From Fatwa to Jihad: The Rushdie Affair and its Legacy* (Atlantic Books, 2009)

L. Mucchielli, 'Autumn 2005: A Review of the Most Important Riot in the History of French Contemporary Society', *Journal of Ethnic and Migration Studies*, 35(5) (2009): 731–51

H. Ouseley, *Community Pride Not Prejudice* (Bradford Vision, 2001)

C. Peach, 'Does Britain Have Ghettoes?', *Transactions of the Institute of British Geographers*, New Series 22 (1996): 216–35

D. Phillips, 'Parallel Lives? Challenging Discourses of British Muslim Self-Segregation', *Environment and Planning D: Society and Space*, 24 (2006): 25–40

D. Ritchie, *One Oldham, One Future* (Oldham Independent Review, 2001)

P. Sniderman and L. Hagendoorn, *When Ways of Life Collide: Multiculturalism and its Discontents in the Netherlands* (Princeton University Press, 2007)

J. Solomos and L. Back, *Race, Politics and Social Change* (Routledge, 1995)

A. Touraine, *Can We Live Together? Equality and Difference* (1997) (Polity Press, 2000)

Chapter 4

B. Arneil, *Diverse Communities: The Problem with Social Capital* (Cambridge University Press, 2006)

L. Back, *New Ethnicities and Urban Culture: Racisms and Multiculture in Young Lives* (UCL Press, 1996)

K. Banting and W. Kymlicka, 'Canada, Not America', *Prospect*, March 2004

K. Banting and W. Kymlicka, 'Multiculturalism and the Welfare State: Setting the Context', in K. Banting and W. Kymlicka (eds.), *Multiculturalism and the Welfare State: Recognition and Redistribution in Contemporary Democracies* (Oxford University Press, 2006)

T. Blair, 'Britishness and Multiculturalism', http://www.telegraph.co. uk/news/migrationtemp/1536354/Full-text-of Blairs-multiculturalism-speech

S. Clarke, R. Gilmour, and S. Garner, 'Home, Identity and Community Cohesion', in M. Wetherell, M. Lafleche, and R. Berkeley (eds.), *Identity, Ethnic Diversity and Community Cohesion* (Sage, 2007)

S. Clarke, S. Garner, and R. Gilmour, 'Imagining the Other/Figuring Encounter: White English Middle Class and Working Class Identifications', in M. Wetherell (ed.), *Identity in the 21st Century: New Trends in Changing Times* (Palgrave Macmillan, 2009)

Commission on Integration and Cohesion, *Our Shared Future* (Commission on Integration and Cohesion, 2007)

G. Dench, K. Gavron, and M. Young, *The New East End: Kinship, Race and Conflict* (Profile Books, 2006)

R. Forrest and A. Kearns, 'Social Cohesion, Social Capital and the Neighbourhood', *Urban Studies* 38(12) 2001: 2125–43

S. Garner, 'Home Truths: The White Working Class and the Racialization of Social Housing', in K. Sveinsson (ed.), *Who Cares about the White Working Class?* (Runnymede Trust, 2009)

K. Gavron, 'Acknowledged Identities: A Common Endeavour or Wider Hostilities', in M. Wetherell, M. Lafleche, and R. Berkeley (eds.), *Identity, Ethnic Diversity and Community Cohesion* (Sage, 2007)

A. Gilchrist, *Community Development and Community Cohesion: Bridges or Barricades?* (Community Development Foundation, 2004)

D. Goodhart, 'Too Diverse?', *Prospect*, February 2004

P. Hall, 'Social Capital in Britain', *British Journal of Political Science*, 28 (1999): 417–61

M. Hickman, H. Crowley, and N. Mai, *Immigration and Social Cohesion in the UK: The Rhythms and Realities of Everyday Life* (Joseph Rowntree Foundation, 2008)

M. Hudson, J. Phillips, K. Ray, and H. Barnes, *Social Cohesion in Diverse Communities* (Joseph Rowntree Foundation, 2007)

M. Keith, 'Between Being and Becoming? Rights, Responsibilities and the Politics of Multiculture in the New East End', *Sociological Research Online*, 13(5) (2008)

N. Letki, 'Does Diversity Erode Social Cohesion? Social Capital and Race in British Neighbourhoods', *Political Studies*, 56: 99–126

R. Moore, 'Careless Talk: A Critique of Dench, Gavron and Young's *The New East End*', *Critical Social Policy*, 28(3) (2008): 349–60

B. Parekh, 'What Are Civilized Rules?', *Prospect*, March 2004

R. Putnam, *Bowling Alone: The Collapse and Revival of American Community* (Simon and Schuster, 2000)

R. Putnam and L. Feldstein, *Better Together: Restoring the American Community* (Simon and Schuster, 2003)

A. Rattansi, 'Who's British?: *Prospect* and the New Assimilationism', in R. Berkeley (ed.), *Cohesion, Community and Citizenship* (Runnymede Trust, 2002)

P. Taylor-Gooby, 'Is the Future American? Or, Can Left Politics Preserve European Welfare States from Erosion through Growing "Racial" Diversity?', *Journal of Social Policy*, 34(4) (2005): 661–72

R. Zetter, D. Griffiths, N. Sigona, D. Flynn, T. Pasha, and R. Beynon, *Immigration, Social Cohesion and Social Capital: What Are the Links?* (Joseph Rowntree Foundation, 2006)

Chapter 5

K. Ajebgo, *Diversity and Citizenship: Curriculum Review* (DfES, 2007)

M. Alam (ed.), *Made in Bradford* (Route Books, 2008)

C. Alexander, *The Art of Being Black* (Oxford University Press, 1996)

P. Bagguley and Y. Hussain (eds.), *Riotous Citizens: Ethnic Conflict in Multicultural Britain* (Ashgate, 2008)

R. Ballard (ed.), *Desh Pardesh: The South Asian Presence in Britain* (Hurst, 1994)

T. Blair, 'Multiculturalism and Britishness', (www.telegraph.co.uk/news, 9 December 2006)

G. Brown, 'The Future of Britishness', Speech at the Fabian Britishness Conference, 14 January 2006, http://www. fabiansociety.org.uk/press_office/news)

C. Caldwell, *Reflections on the Revolution in Europe: Immigration, Islam and the West* (Allen Lane, 2009)

L. Colley, *Britishness in the 21st Century* (Millenium Lecture, London School of Economics and Foreign and Commonwealth Office, 1999)

R. Colls, 'In Search of British Values', *Prospect*, October 2007

J. Esposito and D. Mogahed, *Who Speaks for Islam? What a Billion Muslims Really Believe* (Gallup Press, 2007)

M. Farrar, 'Leeds Footsoldiers and London Bombs', <http://www. OpenDemocracy.net>, 21 July 2005

S. Glyn, 'Bengali Muslims: The New East End Radicals?', *Ethnic and Racial Studies*, 23(6) (2002): 969–88

A. Heath, J. Martin, and G. Elgenius, 'Who Do We Think We Are? The Decline of Traditional Identities', in A. Park (ed.), *British Social Attitudes: The 23rd Report* (Sage, 2007)

E. Hobsbawm, 'In Search of British Values', *Prospect*, October 2007

Home Office and Foreign and Commonwealth Office, *Young Muslims and Extremism* (www.times-archive.co.uk/online specials/cabinet.pdf

S. Huntington, *The Clash of Civilizations and the Remaking of the World Order* (Simon and Schuster, 1996)

W. Laquer, *The Last Days of Europe: Epitaph for an Old Continent* (Thomas Dunne, 2007)

A. Lentin, 'The Intifada of the Banlieues', <http://www. OpenDemocracy.net>, 17 November 2005

P. Lewis, *Young, British and Muslim* (Continuum, 2007)

S. Malik, 'My Brother the Bomber: The Inside Story of 7/7 Leader Mohammad Siddique Khan', *Prospect*, June 2007

D. Marquand, ' "Bursting with Skeletons": Britishness after Empire', in A. Gamble and T. Wright (eds.), *Britishness: Perspectives on the Britishness Question* (Wiley-Blackwell, 2009)

A. Mondal, *Young British Muslim Voices* (Greenwood, 2008)

A. Rattansi, 'On Being and Not Being Brown/Black British: Racism, Class and Sexuality in Post-Imperial Britain', in J.-A. Lee and J. Lutz (eds.), *Situating 'Race' and Racisms in Time, Space, and Theory* (Queen's Unversity Press, 2005)

O. Roy, *Globalised Islam: The Search for a New Ummah* (2002) (Columbia University Press, 2004)

D. Watson, 'Citizenship Lessons "Nationalistic and Politically Skewed"', <http://www.timesonline.co.uk/tolnews/uk/education/article5476080>

F. Zakaria, 'The Jihad against the Jihadis: How Moderate Muslim Leaders Waged War on Extremists – and Won', *Newsweek*, 22 February 2010

S. Zubaida, 'Is There a Muslim Society?', *Economy and Society*, 24(2) (1995): 151–88

S. Zubaida, 'The London Bombs: Iraq or the "Rage of Islam"?', <http://www.OpenDeomcracy.net>, 2 August 2005

Conclusion

A. Amin, 'Ethnicity and the Multicultural City: Living with Diversity', *Environment and Planning A*, 34 (2002): 959–80

'Bagehot', 'In Praise of Multiculturalism', *The Economist*, 16 June 2007

M. Bernal, *Black Athena: The Afro-Asiatic Roots of Classical Civilization* (Free Association Books, 1987)

A. Giddens, 'Misunderstanding Multiculturalism', *The Guardian*, 14 October 2006

N. Glazer, *We Are All Multiculturalists Now* (Harvard University Press, 1997)

J. Goody, *The East in the West* (Cambridge University Press, 1996)

J. Goody, *The Theft of History* (Cambridge University Press, 2006)

J. Goody, *The Eurasian Miracle* (Polity Press, 2010)

R. Grillo, *Contesting Diversity in Europe: Alternative Regimes and Moral Orders* (Max Planck Institute MMG Working Paper 10_02, 2010)

M. Hewstone, N. Tausch, J. Hughes, and E. Cairns, 'Prejudice, Intergroup Contact and Identity: Do Neighbourhoods Matter?', in M. Wetherell, M. Lafleche, and R. Berkeley (eds.), *Identity, Ethnic Diversity and Community Cohesion* (Sage, 2007)

D. Hibbert, 'Cosmopolitanism at the Local Level: The Development of Transnational Neighbourhoods', in S. Vertovec and R. Cohen (eds.), *Conceiving Cosmopolitanism: Theory, Context and Practice* (Oxford University Press, 2002)

D. Hollinger, *Postethnic America: Beyond Multiculturalism*, 2nd edn. (Basic Books, 2000)

C. Mouffe, 'Democracy, Power and the "Political"', in S. Benhabib (ed.), *Democracy and Difference: Contesting the Boundaries of the Political* (Princeton University Press, 1996)

B. Parekh, *Rethinking Multiculturalism: Liberalism and Cultural Diversity*, 2nd edn. (Palgrave Macmillan, 2005)

B. Parekh, *A New Politics of Identity: Political Principles for an Interdependent World* (Palgrave Macmillan, 2008)

Runnymede Trust Commission, *The Future of Multi-Ethnic Britain* (Profile Books, 2000)

A. Schachar, *Multicultural Jurisdictions: Cultural Differences and Women's Rights* (Cambridge University Press, 2001)

K. Schmid, M. Hewstone, J. Hughes, R. Jenkins, and E. Cairns, 'Residential Segregation and Intergroup Contact: Consequences for Intergroup Relations, Social Capital and Social Identity', in M. Wetherell (ed.), *Theorizing Identities and Social Action* (Palgrave Macmillan, 2009)

A. Sen, 'Culture and Human Rights', in his *Development as Freedom* (Oxford University Press, 1999)

A. Sen, *The Argumentative Indian: Writings on Indian History, Culture and Identity* (Picador, 2005)

J. Tully, 'Struggles over Recognition and Redistribution', *Constellations*, 7(4) (2000): 469–82

J. Tully, 'Recognition and Dialogue: The Emergence of a New Field', *Critical Review of International Social and Political Philosophy*, 7(3) (2004): 84–106

A. Varshney, *Ethnic Conflict and Civic Life: Hindus and Muslims in India*, 2nd edn. (Yale University Press, 2003)

S. Vertovec and S. Wessendorf (eds.), *The Multiculturalism Backlash: European Discourses, Policies and Practices* (Routledge, 2010)

P. Wood and C. Henry, *The Intercultural City: Planning for Diversity Advantage* (Earthscan, 2008)

Further reading

Chapter 1

R. Hewitt, *White Backlash and the Politics of Multiculturalism* (Cambridge University Press, 2005)

W. Kymlicka and B. He (eds.), *Multiculturalism in Asia* (Oxford University Press, 2005)

Chapter 2

S. Benhabib, *The Claims of Culture: Equality and Diversity in a Global Era* (Princeton University Press, 2002)

Chapter 3

S. Body-Gendrot, 'Police Marginality, Racial Logics and Discrimination in the *Banlieues* of France', *Ethnic and Racial Studies*, 33 (4) (2009): 656–74

Chapter 4

J. Flint and D. Robinson (eds.), *Community Cohesion in Crisis?* (Policy Press, 2008)

Chapter 5

J. Cesari, *When Islam and Democracy Meet: Muslims in Europe and the US* (Palgrave Macmillan, 2004)

J. Klausen, *The Cartoons that Shook the World* (Yale University Press, 2009)

T. Modood, A. Trandafyllidou, and R. Zapata (eds.), *Multiculturalism, Muslims and Citizenship: A European Approach* (Routledge, 2006)

S. Saggar, *Pariah Politics: Understanding Western Islamic Radicalism and What Should Be Done* (Oxford University Press, 2009)

Conclusion

Y. Alibhai-Brown, *After Multiculturalism* (Foreign Policy Centre, 2000)

K. Bhambra, *Rethinking Modernity: Postcolonialism and the Sociological Imagination* (Palgrave Macmillan, 2007)

W. Brown, *Regulating Aversion: Tolerance in the Age of Identity and Empire* (Princeton University Press, 2006)

S. Hall, 'The Multicultural Question', in B. Hesse (ed.), *Un/settled Multiculturalisms* (Zed Press, 2000)

J. Hobson, *The Eastern Origins of Western Civilization* (Cambridge University Press, 2004)

R. Wilkinson and K. Pickett, *The Spirit Level: Why More Equal Societies Almost Always Do Better* (Allen Lane, 2009)

Index

Multiculturalism